There's Always a Bull Market

There's Always a Bull Market
Conservative Investing in Stocks, Bonds, and Gold

Robert Kinsman

Dow Jones-Irwin
Homewood, Illinois 60430

Project editor: Jane Lightell
Production manager: Ann Cassady
Jacket designer: Michael S. Finkelman
Compositor: Publication Services
Typeface: 11/13 Century Schoolbook
Printer: Arcata Graphics/Kingsport

Library of Congress Cataloging-in-Publication Data

Kinsman, Robert.
    There's always a bull market: conservative investing in stocks, bonds, and gold / Robert Kinsman.
    p. cm.
    ISBN 1-55623-186-5
    1. Investments—United States. 2. Stocks—United States.
3. Bonds—United States. 4. Gold—United States. I. Title.
HG4521.K478   1990   89–37610
332.63'0973—dc20   CIP

Printed in the United States of America
1 2 3 4 5 6 7 8 9 0 K 6 5 4 3 2 1 0 9

*For Dad, with the wish that
in all our 85th years, we'll
be able to outscore our kids in golf.*

INTRODUCTION

Financial author Andrew Tobias told me a story a few years ago while we were waiting for a television interview crew in his room at San Francisco's posh Huntington Hotel. It seems a foreign professor of his at business school recommended one book as must reading for every student. It was the 143-year-old tome that he said was called "Extraordinary Popular Delusions and the Madness of Krauts."[1]

Tobias said he wondered for days why the Germans were called Krauts back in the 1840s and whether the author had really used that nickname in the title. Upon buying the book, he discovered the word was *Crowds*.

Tobias found this story so germane to understanding investing that he included it in his introduction to the 1980 reprint of the book.

In a real sense "crowds" is what my book is all about: what crowds of investors do and when you should part company from them.

Extraordinary Popular Delusions focuses on the manias with which investors become enamored, including the tulip bulb craze in Holland and the South Sea Islands bubble. Its point is one that can't be stressed enough: periodically, ordinary people come to believe in an investment idea so feverishly that they push it past all reasonable standards of value. Then comes the crash.

Late 1980s investors saw that game played out first-hand. It was the first-ever living room stock market collapse, thanks to television. The bubble burst on the evening news, and one more example of crowd madness went into the record books.

---

[1] *Extraordinary Popular Delusions and The Madness of Crowds* by Charles Mackay was most recently published in 1980 by Harmony Books, New York. It was first published under the title "Memoirs of Extraordinary Popular Delusions" in 1841.

But investors following just part of the method I'll describe in this volume were barely fazed by the October 1987 Crash. They knew as early as the previous May that the game was ending and were advised to raise substantial cash: 70 percent of portfolio. Four days before October 19, they knew a major bear market had begun. These investors had departed from the crowd to their real benefit.

So what happened *after* the bubble went kaput? Did the crowd return to sanity in the form of seeking out reasonable value in other investments? Not on your life. In 1988 they turned in one of two directions: to futures markets, where the risk was statistically up to 40 times that of stocks, or to nothing. *Hand-sitting* was the second alternative's apt description.

Ignoring the futures casino for the moment, let's look at the other idea, sitting tight. The Crash, of course, did destroy a lot of confidence in stocks, stock advisors, and money managers. It was a valid reason for becoming cautious.

But there were other factors playing themselves out along with that wariness. Many investors were sitting not only on their hands but also on substantial stock positions. Most didn't realize that while the history of stock market crashes shows almost automatic important rallies in the ensuing six months or sometimes a year, that history also verifies that the next true stock bull market almost never starts within a year, and usually not within 18 months of the crash. And long bear swipes last over three years. Why hold stocks all through what could be a nasty long spell?

There are reasons, of course. Many investors were holding stocks with substantial losses. Others still had large capital gains. Those are at least arguable reasons for continuing to hold stocks. And hindsight shows that for the first time in crash history at least a minimum bull market in stocks did begin in December after the '87 crash. So, *some* might have expected that. But darn few in my experience.

The question is, should most stocks be *automatically* held if you know that while there's a potential for a nasty bear market still ahead, a bull market in either bonds or gold was historically "just around the corner"? Shouldn't investors be looking there? Shrewd investors found the bull in bonds that charged forth in fall of 1987.

Yes, that's precisely what market history says. The fact is that in *every single year* of the past 40 years, there has been a bull market[*] underway in U.S. stocks, or bonds, or gold mining stocks. No exceptions. Every calendar year in the modern investing era witnessed a bull market in one or more of those three arenas.

That's not all. We can go back as far as I have records for all three markets—1923. Would you believe there was a bull market in force in every year from then until 1939? Right through the Great Depression? The Depression was a myth if you were invested in the *right market*. This means investors could have nearly always invested in bull markets (1947 also saw a gap) since the administration of President Warren Harding!

Wait a minute, you say. Certainly *continuous* bull markets weren't in force for the past 65 years, even with three markets to choose from? You're right. There were gaps. But the statement that a bull market existed in every *calendar* year through the Depression and for the past 40 years, is true.

Specifically, from 1948 through 1988, intra-year bull market gaps occurred on average less than once a *decade*, and lasted an average of only eight months. The proof is in Figure I–1.

The only two breaks in the whole 65 years that were longer than a year bracketed World War II: 1939–41 and 1946–47.

What's more, every one of those interruptions was caused by the Federal Reserve Board changing monetary conditions. No exceptions.

All of this is strong stuff. I'd guess that not one investor in 20 is aware of it, including most professionals. When I asked a question about this at my April 1988 Low-Risk GROWTH Letter seminar in San Francisco, only one in five attendees even came close. The question was, "Over the past *20 years*, how many years saw a bull market in either stocks, bonds, or gold?" Choices were 8–12 years, 13–16 years, or 17–20 years. Eighty percent of the attendees chose the first two periods. One man got the answer right: all 20 years.

---

[*] My definition of a bull market excludes moderate rallies: It is a rising market that shows a *25 percent or greater gain in average prices* from the bottom month to those in the peak month.

FIGURE I–1

A Bull Market Every Year, 1948–1989. (Gains of 25% or more, on average prices in months shown).

	Hindsight Bull Markets	
Nov. '48 to Nov. '49:	Gold Stocks	+31.0%
Jun. '49 to Jul. '57:	S& P 500	+248.9%
Jul. '50 to Aug. '52:	Gold Stocks	+43.0%
Dec. '53 to Jun. '57:	Gold Stocks	+63.0%
Oct. '57 to Dec. '59:	S&P 500	+46.0%
Dec. '57 to Mar. '69:	Gold Stocks	+331.0%
Oct. '60 to Dec. '61:	S&P 500	+33.5%
Jun. '62 to Jan. '66:	S& P 500	+67.7%
Oct. '66 to Dec. '68:	S&P 500	+38.1%
Dec. '69 to Apr. '71:	Gold Stocks	+64.0%
Jun. '70 to Jan. '73:	S& P 500	+56.6%
Dec. '71 to Aug. '74:	Gold Stocks	+349.0%
Dec. '74 to Jan. '77:	S&P 500	+56.4%
Mar. '78 to Nov. '80:	S&P 500	+52.6%
Nov. '78 to Oct. '80:	Gold Stocks	+372.0%
Feb. '80 to Jun. '80:	Bonds	+26.8%
Sep. '81 to Nov. '82:	Bonds	+47.4%
Jun. '82 to May '83:	Gold Stocks	+201.0%
Aug. '82 to Aug. '87:	S&P 500	+197.2%
Nov. '83 to Mar. '84:	Gold Stocks	+26.0%
Jun. '84 to Apr. '87:	Bonds	+80.5%
Jan. '85 to Aug. '85:	Gold Stocks	+25.0%
Jul. '86 to Sep. '87:	Gold Stocks	+191.0%
Dec. '87 to May. '89:	S&P 500	+27.2%

Those are the facts that much of the investment crowd was ignoring in the post-crash world of 1988. Most weren't getting ready for a new bull market among our three by looking for incipient bull market conditions, studying market values, identifying new trends, or even setting buying price limits. I guess they didn't believe a new bull was just around the corner.

Much of the crowd was being deluded again.

Fortunately, you don't wish to be part of that crowd. You're reading this book with what I hope is the idea that you'll find a new approach to your investments. That's certainly my goal.

So exactly what is this new information going to do for you?

First, the facts alone should tell you that by considering just three markets—stocks, bonds, and gold—you can expect to be invested for capital growth almost all the time. Over 92 percent of the time in the past two decades in fact.

Second, you can take my word for it now that the Federal Reserve is the key player in determining when the bull markets start and stop. I'll show you why and how.

Third, the results are significant in following this Right Market Method (RMM) of investing. Since all the market indicators I'll show you were operable in free markets—the 22 years through 1988, on a back-tested basis—the total compounded gain from investing with our indicator signals in all three markets aggregated 2993.3 percent, and this did *not* include dividends or interest on cash during the intra-year gaps. This compares to a buy-and-hold gain in the S&P 500 of just 256 percent. The Right Market Method produces!

The best part about the Right Market Method is that it can be used by any investor. It's not complicated. For example, you'll just need to invest in *one* no-load mutual fund (or individual stocks and bonds if you prefer) for each bull market.

And, you won't need to trade in and out frequently either. In the most active market of the past 22 years, stocks, this investing method called for just eight buy-sell switches: 16 transactions. (There was an additional buy and sell in 1989).

RMM is not speculative. It allows for risk control at every step and advises that you make your lowest risk investments at critical turning points: as bull markets begin and end.

In addition, RMM is not a "trend-following" approach. It's anticipatory of market trends. It doesn't require a market move to get underway before saying "go." It sends signals when the underlying *conditions* for a bull market turn right or wrong, no matter whether other investors know it or not.

What about *income investors*, those who need to live on their investment income? No problem. You'll invest in stocks paying high dividends during the stock bull markets, or in long-term bonds during their bull phases. This should generate capital growth along with income. During gold bull markets, we'll use money market funds, Treasury bills (T-bills), and Treasury notes (T-notes) of one to three year maturities. The special rules for income investors are included in the specific chapters on each market.

The most important point is that all this works because there's a *secret* behind the Right Market Method. It's the simplest secret in the world. It's called price inflation-deflation. It's obvious that prices can only do three things: go up, go down, or stay unchanged. That's true of the economy, too. It can only grow, decline, or stagnate. Those three simple alternatives create this investment method. That's because each of these possibilities has a market that *optimizes* its trend: Gold performs best at times when inflation accelerates, bonds do best in periods when prices decelerate or actually decline, and the stock market shows its best gains during times of moderate economic growth and moderate price changes. One of our three markets fits each of the three economic/price conditions that can exist at any time.

Put another way, if one of only three price/economic conditions can exist at any one time, and each has a single market that best reflects that condition, there should always be a market riding the existing condition: a bull wave. The only conceivable times when this might not be true is when the markets are unsure of which condition is operable, or during transitions from one condition to another. And those times are historically very rare, as we've seen.

That's it. That's the secret behind the Right Market Method.

Now, the problem with this for investors, if they indeed knew the facts, is that until this moment there has been no *single* investment approach that exploited this three-market "secret." The Right Market Method thus creates *the first true asset allocation investment approach that's based on the inflation-deflation cycle.*

After 28 years as an investment pro, I'm not given to hyperbole. I've seen too many "systems" come and go, along with their proponents. Let me assure you there is reality here.

What excites me about this method is that is combines both theory and hard evidence over a sufficient number of market cycles to be statistically significant. And since I've actually used part of it for a decade, I know it really works.

Bull markets are going to repeat with similar regularity to those of the past several decades. The only question is whether you'll be ready for them.

If you'd like to get prepared and learn how to easily use this investment method through my "SIMPL" set of market indicators, this book is for you.

CONTENTS

There's Always a
Bull Market

CHAPTER 1

THE WHISTLING LEMON EFFECT

> The only thing we learn from history is that we do not learn
> from history.—*Milton Friedman*

Dramatic changes in the investment markets are hallmarks of investing in the 1980s. Computerized program trading, asset allocation strategies, and instant FAX dissemination of advice are realities today. Almost no investors knew about them a decade ago.

A long-term investment approach that I've named the Right Market Method (RMM) enables you to anticipate changes in the markets themselves and act with certainty to reach your personal investment targets. RMM is the asset allocation discipline that provides capital growth potential *and* risk control. Mostly importantly, it allows you to identify which market is likely to be in a bull phase every year in the future just as it has over the past four decades. To see how, we must first deal with the problems of rapid market changes.

British journalist and historian James Burke has gained a measure of fame over the past decade by hosting a pair of PBS television series and authoring books based on them. His *Connections* and *The Day the Universe Changed* were seen by large audiences, and both the series and books received critical acclaim.

The viewpoint of *Universe* is an intriguing one. It's that truth is simply what we perceive it to be. It is not absolute, immutable, and awaiting discovery. It's relative. "You see what you want to see," in the words of philosopher Wittgenstein. Thus, as Burke says, whenever an important truth is altered, the universe we know also changes.

While he was on tour promoting that TV series and book, Burke gave a speech in San Francisco that had something to do with "whistling lemons." I don't recall the full title, and didn't hear his remarks, but the idea of a whistling lemon seemed so unreal that it got me to thinking. After reading *Universe* (in which there was no reference to whistling lemons, by the way), it occurred to me that whistling lemons had a direct applicability to investments. In fact, they can be most useful in understanding what's happening to the investment world right now. They dramatically emphasize one problem that technology is creating for the investment decision process, one which investors must face: the increased speed with which market changes are occurring.

To understand my solution to the problem, we need to know a bit about Burke's ideas. Is he right? Is truth relative?

First, historical examples abound of truth being what we see it to be. The world is no longer known to be at the center of the universe, nor is it flat. But those beliefs—truths—were dogma for centuries, a lot longer, for example, than we've had a science known as statistics. Galileo and Christopher Columbus gained no small measure of fame in helping prove those "truths" false.

Further, we now believe that a physician knows better what ails a patient than the patient does. But until the beginning of the last century the exact opposite was true. Doctors not only asked patients what bothered them, but took their advice in prescribing cures. It was not until the unlikely combination of wars and statistics joined the advancing science of medicine that the patient-primacy "truth" changed.

Perhaps the most insightful example of truth change comes from something we take absolutely for granted today, but which in fact we still don't fully comprehend: the electron.

In 1927, as Burke relates it, physicist Werner Heisenberg concluded a series of experiments with methods of "seeing" electrons. He was attempting to solve a problem that had bothered scientists since the 18th century: electrons acted like particles of matter one moment and like waves of energy the next.

Heisenberg's work created a new truth that's still believed today: It can never be determined whether electrons are waves or particles because both are products of the instruments used to observe them. One could look for particles and find them, or one could look for waves and find them, but not both at once. The act of observing electrons in action requires shining some form of light on them. This adds to the energy of the electron and alters its state or position.

"If we want to describe what happens in an atomic event," Heisenberg wrote, "we have to realize the word 'happens' can apply only to the observation, not to the state of affairs between observations."

According to Burke, the result of this was no less than to destroy a truth accepted since ancient Greek times: that direct cause and effect always held true. But no more. We see what we want to—or can—see.

Enter the lowly lemon.

What do we know about lemons? Well, they are yellow; have a pretty, sweet flower; carry a bitter juice; and are semi-soft to the touch. When cut open, squeezing causes them to emit both air and juice.

Whistling can be defined as the emission of air and sound from an opening by either an animate or inanimate object. The act of whistling does not require carrying a tune, or we wouldn't have whistling tea kettles.

From these "truths" we know that lemons do not whistle. The sound is missing from lemon squeezing.

But we must ask if we could prove the contrary: Is there a sound that could be measured? I'd say that proving this requires (a) a serious focus on the question, (b) defining how low a level of sound emission we accept as whistling, and (c) putting some effort into studying squeezed lemon emissions. It also depends on our ability to measure the sound of those emissions.

Proof will *not* depend on the existence of some immutable truth that lemons cannot whistle. That's only what we believe at our present state of knowledge (and interest).

At this point you're probably wondering what all this has to do with investments. Simply that investments must reflect the process of changing what we believe as truth. If truth-facts change, investments based on them must change also.

Until xerography was invented, there existed no high-definition method of precise image reproduction of printed pages. When the Haloid Xerox Corporation was formed to exploit this changed truth, a new investment was born. And with it, a whole industry of competitors for those investment dollars was created.

No one can deny that the product world is changing rapidly. In widely used consumer goods alone over the past 15 years we've become accustomed to video recorders, laptop computers, microwave ovens, electronic typewriters, and hundreds of other products that couldn't exist until the new facts on which they're based were uncovered. Changed product "truth" is now a way of life.

And does anyone really doubt that the speed of such changes is increasing? Alvin Toffler first articulated that idea in popular print nearly two decades ago in *Future Shock*. I doubt that anyone seriously questions it any longer.

In fact, it is arguably a goal of Western society to promote change. Would we be teaching our children to use increasingly sophisticated computers and snapping up the fastest, most powerful small versions of them for our business and personal use if this weren't true? Or is it not true that computers create change? Try discussing computer functions with your kids IF you don't already use a computer. The language is as foreign as Russian is to English. They're learning it and you probably didn't. That's certainly a change.

Or consider the conclusions of a study conducted at the University of Wales Institute of Science and Technology on human response to computer speech patterns. The Sunday *Times* of London reported that "users [people] modified their responses to correspond with the computer's approach. If it communicated by speech, but used staccato commands, users tended to bark back at it. But when it spoke in a natural, friendly manner with a good number of 'encouraging phrases,' users responded by using relaxed, normal tones and language."

I suppose there aren't many of us who've been "encouraged" by computer language. So far.

The sum of all this tells me that change must be a goal of society. Perhaps it's de facto, if not purposeful, but it's a goal nonetheless. If it wasn't, we'd be trying to stop the changes. Instead, we welcome them.

Back to investments. If they reflect product and service changes, they also bring an added element to the change process: *speculation*. Investments are made not only in proven products or those just announced, but also in those rumored or expected to be announced. The biotechnology industry is comprised of a significant number of companies whose stocks move in price largely on the anticipated value of products that are now merely being studied or tested.

It follows then that investment opportunities and investment prices must change at least as rapidly, and faster in some instances, than the anticipated changes in product concepts or the products/services themselves. Investments must be at the vanguard of the increasing speed of change in facts we know to be true. Investments lead the way.

If we look a bit further, we see that not only are investments changing in this way, but the number of investment vehicles is also exploding. Twenty years ago there were no money market funds, publicly traded liquid CDs, long-term zero coupon bonds, GNMAs or FNMAs, or master limited partnerships, to name a few. More types are on the way right now.

The point I'm making is that we can use the whistling lemon—the possibility that it *could* exist—as an unusual reminder of how, and potentially how fast, the world of truth (and the investment process in it) is changing.

So far, we humans seem to be capable of handling this crush of change in society and how we invest in it. But, considering the dramatic alterations in family structure and personal relationships and the massive psychiatric and drug problems society is developing, one suspects that our capacity to absorb change may be related to these massive upsets. Since most of these problems appear to reflect an inability to cope with society, why wouldn't society's faster and faster changes be related to the problems? Are not computerized stock/futures trading problems during the Crash of '87 the investment industry's version of too fast a speed of change?

Whatever the case, it's another story. The fact remains that investing in the present level of change in society requires each investor to face a difficult problem: either increase the speed of the investment decision process to match that of the changes, or find a process that will work within the time frame of any speed of change. What's more, delaying a decision is, in fact, making a decision to be bypassed, in my opinion. Failing to cope with change is to be overrun in the investment world.

If you doubt the need for a decision on this score, consider how integral the speed of change is to investment prices.

Investment volatility is defined as the speed and magnitude of change in a given investment's price compared to some norm—either to the "market" as a whole, or to its own trendline, or to a separate index. With stocks the measurement is usually to the Standard & Poor's 500, a proxy for the overall market.

Now, any new product or service announcement must create a new factor in its company's stock price. It may be a large factor in small companies and a small factor in large firms, but it's new and it's a factor to some degree. Anything that forces a change in a stock price will increase that stock's volatility pattern—again varying by company. And the many new product/service arrivals at a faster and faster pace must have the effect of increasing the *market's* overall volatility, all other factors being equal. From this fact we cannot escape.

Couldn't we sidestep that increased volatility by just choosing less volatile stocks? Yes, but with a penalty. That means staying away from the most innovative companies, an idea that doesn't make much sense for growth-oriented investors. And, if that is done, the reduced volatility will mean reduced potential for gains in rising markets. It is volatility that, in part, produces better *gains* in rising markets.

So we can avoid the volatility problem by paying the piper to deal with it, not by totally escaping it.

But, all is not lost to those of us who prefer not to become day traders in stocks or stock indexes, or who don't want to invest only in stodgy companies. I said earlier that we have a choice in this matter. We can locate an investment process that will work within the time frame of any speed of change. Fortunately, there is a way. It involves making use of the biggest cushion to fast change in the financial world—the Federal Reserve Board.

The Fed, as everybody calls it, functions as a cushion to change not because it's opposed to innovation, but because it's just plain slow. The Fed carries out its principal roles as defender of the currency and lender of last resort by normally taking months, not minutes, to put a policy into effect and to review its results. That's snail-like.

Since our markets react significantly to nearly all overt actions by the Fed (or what they believe it will do), not to what they think it *should* do to accommodate change, we have a ready-made shock absorber. This gives thoughtful investors plenty of time to act, *if* they have the right indicators of Fed actions.

We'll deal further with the Fed in upcoming chapters, but for now it's enough to recognize that the Fed acts slowly for four main reasons.

1. The economic statistics on which it acts take time to gather and publish. Most data are issued a month after being compiled, sometimes two.
2. Those numbers are subject to revision, often substantial revision. Usually another month disappears with this.
3. When the Fed has "good" numbers, it may act to put a policy into effect by trading in the short-term money market or by announcing a rate or regulation change. This follows a meeting of appropriate Fed officials which itself may absorb anywhere from a few hours to a few weeks.
4. The policy must then be reviewed for effect, a process that can take up to several additional months.

Even in steps 1 through 3, the time it takes to know with some certainty what is happening in the economy until the Fed acts rarely passes faster than a few weeks. And this delay hasn't changed notably in the nearly three decades I've been in the financial business. A rare exception was immediately following the 1987 Crash, when the Fed turned on the monetary spigot within a day. The need for action was both psychologically and pragmatically obvious. The Fed *can* act quickly. But the rule remains. It rarely rushes because the data-reporting and action process is simply time-consuming. And the Fed is outrageously cautious. You'd expect that from a central bank.

In sum, our "whistling lemons" are a mnemonic for the reason we need to look to the Fed to capitalize on investments:

to buffer the speed of change in "truth" so we can deal with it in a thoughtful way. A second reason is better known: The Fed's actions are far and away the most critical in causing changes in financial market trends. These two facts create a compelling argument for paying very close attention to Fed actions. I'll show you exactly how to do that in a way that pulls the wheat from the chaff.

Let's now turn to establishing the correct framework for our Right Market Method. Our first step is to understand certain realities in our markets and what we can honestly expect from them.

CHAPTER 2

MARKET REALITY

A study of economics usually reveals that the best time to
buy anything is last year.—*Marty Allen*

Mr. Allen knew his economics: 20/20 hindsight beats forecasting. But the goal of any investment book worth its salt is to
prepare investors for future trends, not the past. That is indeed
what we'll endeavor to do here. Having said that, we must
undertake a little of what Allen referred to. We've got to study
some of the past in order to understand what the future will
bring. We've got to know why "there's always a bull market"—
both past and future.

The reality of the three markets we're addressing—general
stocks, bonds, and gold—is clear. They've combined to create
a nearly continuous bull market for over 40 years. And with a
few longer gaps, that's also been true for an additional 25 years.

This suggests that we have three questions to deal with in
putting this information to work.

1. How probable is it that this phenomenon will continue
   in the future?
2. How can we precisely identify succeeding bull markets
   with good probabilities of success?
3. How should we participate in each bull trend?

We'll address the first point in this chapter.

To start, we'd better agree on exactly what we mean by a
bull market.

Surprisingly, the securities business, the one that has pro-
moted the words *bullish* and *bearish* into our lexicon, has also
given us no standard definition for either bull or bear markets,

other than that bull markets rise and bear markets drop. Ah, precision!

Obviously, the easiest way to decide what has constituted bull and bear markets is to look at the historical record to locate market tops and bottoms for each cycle, and to then decide on a minimum gain that avoids calling every rally a bull market. This is a useful first cut. Its problem, of course, is that it would require omniscience to invest with that approach in the future.

A second course brings the answer down to earth: We can determine what market indicators would have best identified bull and bear phases for each of our three markets. Then we can compare the two approaches with each other. This should be revealing as to how practical the indicators truly are.

Okay. What should be the minimum cutoff percentage for bull and bear markets on a hindsight basis? How much of a gain or loss will adequately filter bull and bear markets from moderate swings?

For this I've selected a percentage gain that takes in all the obvious bull markets in gold, gold mining stocks, general stocks, and bonds since the first bull market after World War II. It does eliminate a few moderate rallies that might be arguable, such as that in 1978, which got nowhere until 1980. A 25 percent minimum gain from cyclical low to high is a sound criterion for a viable bull market. That's neither so large as to miss identifying moderate bull markets, nor so small as to catch mainly short-term rallies.

Further, I've used *average monthly* prices in measuring 25 percent upswings in all markets.

Using these instead of daily or weekly closes clips off market extremes and makes the 25 percent criterion tougher. For example, the Standard & Poor's 500 Index gained 39 percent from its December 1987 daily low to its April 1989 peak. But the average prices in those two months saw only slightly more than one-half that rise, and disqualified that rally as a true bull market by the latter date. (It qualified in May.)

The 25 percent limit itself presents a problem with the bond market, where such bull markets are exceptions rather than the rule. For instance, there was none of that magnitude from 1946 to 1980. As it turns out, this didn't create a problem with our every-year bull market idea; stocks and gold picked up the slack during that long bond drought. Our stern criterion can still apply. There was a 25 percent or greater bull market underway in every calendar year from 1948 through 1988.

This raises the question of corrections in longer-term bull markets. What constitutes a "correction" and how is it differentiated from a full *bear* market? One is tempted to use the same number, 25 percent, from peak to trough as the definition of a bear market, that is, to call bulls and bears equally. The difficulty is whether we can accept a decline of say, 20 percent to 24 percent as just a "correction." Losing over 20 percent of one's invested capital is not just an adjustment in my way of thinking. At the same time, there ought to be some bull market interruption that *does* qualify as a correction without being defined as a bear market. Shouldn't a bull market with a 40 percent gain, for example, be accorded greater dignity than calling a 15 percent decline a full bear market?

Since there is again no formal standard in the industry, I've arbitrarily selected 20 percent as the cutoff. It's a round number below which I think most market professionals would be comfortable terming the drop as a correction, and above which we clearly have a market decline of note. The same cutoff also applies to corrections in bear markets.

So, my rules for bull and bear market identification in reviewing market history are that a bull market constitutes a 25 percent or greater rise from bottom to top, as identified in the market records of monthly average prices. A bear market is any decline of 20 percent or more on the same basis. Corrections are then those countertrend moves of less than 25 percent or 20 percent, respectively.

Naturally, you're quite free to apply your own criteria to the records and draw your own conclusions.

Following are the bull market gains of 25 percent or more since 1948, arranged by market, with a special consideration for bonds. Gains shown are from the average price in the beginning month to the average price in the concluding month. Interest and dividends are not included. These are the "hindsight" bull markets, not those the Right Market Method has invested in.

Stocks: (S&P Composite). The 1942–46 bull market ended in May 1946. After that,

June 1949 to July 1957:	248.9%
October 1957 to December 1959:	46.0%
October 1960 to December 1961:	33.5%
June 1962 to January 1966:	67.7%
October 1966 to December 1968:	38.1%
June 1970 to January 1973:	56.6%
December 1974 to January 1977:	56.4%
March 1978 to November 1980:	52.6%
August 1982 to August 1987:	197.2%

One thousand dollars invested in June 1949 in the S&P Composite and sold in August 1987 would have been worth $23,340, *plus* dividends. Buying and selling the bull markets as shown would have shown a gain of nearly 34.2 *times* that amount, without dividends.

Bonds: (S&P Long-Term Governments). Arguably, there was no bull market in long-term government bonds by our definition from 1946 to 1980. However, if we included the modest bond rallies starting in 1948, the results are:

April 1948 to December 1949:	3.5%
June 1953 to July 1954:	8.3%
October 1957 to April 1958:	12.0%
January to August 1960:	9.3%
June 1970 to November 1973:	21.2%
September 1975 to December 1976:	13.8%
February to June 1980:	26.8%
September 1981 to November 1982:	47.4%
June 1984 to April 1987:	80.5%

One thousand dollars invested in this index in April 1948 and sold in December 1987 would have been worth only $503.10. However, interest paid would have amounted to a considerable sum. And buying/selling the bull markets shown would have created $6,384.78 in principal, or over 12 times more than a buy-hold strategy, without interest.

Gold Mining Stocks: (S&P Gold Mining Index)

November 1948 to November 1949:	31.0%
July 1950 to August 1952:	43.0%
December 1953 to June 1957:	63.0%
December 1957 to March 1969:	331.0%
December 1969 to April 1971:	64.0%
December 1971 to August 1974:	349.0%
November 1978 to October 1980:	372.0%
June 1982 to May 1983:	201.%
November 1983 to March 1984:	26.0%
January 1985 to August 1985:	25.0%
July 1986 to September 1987:	191.0%

One thousand dollars invested in this index in November 1948 and sold in September 1987 would have been worth $58,330, plus dividends. A return of 29.1 *times* that would have rewarded the omniscient investor who bought each bull market low and sold at each high.

A few observations. Our record of consecutive bull markets in every year could have been almost accomplished without the bond market. Note that only one of the gaps, that in 1981, was shortened by bond action. The others were created with almost no help from bonds. However, since the 1949–1987 period was one of generally rising inflation rates and the future need not necessarily be the same, it's prudent to include bonds in our Right Market Method, especially since the evidence of the 1980s shows longer duration bond bull markets than gold bull markets. What's more, our inflation-deflation theory requires bonds to cover the deflation alternative.

Gold mining issues were the clear winners during the last 40-year period, returning more than twice as much as common stocks. What else would we expect in an inflation era? In the low inflation period of the 50s and early 60s, general stocks and gold mining stocks came out very close in gains.

That's the record. But how certain are we that the every-year bull/bear pattern will continue?

THE BIG STICK IN FINANCIAL MARKETS

We don't need to argue whether bull and bear markets will exist in the future. That dichotomy will occur as long as there is a business cycle or a political cycle in the United States. What we're really asking is whether they are likely to continue the every-calendar-year pattern?

I suppose we should next remind ourselves that nothing is certain about the future, except that it will arrive. In that sense, we cannot be certain that our every-year bull market phenomenon will continue to operate.

But, as we've seen, there's very strong historical evidence in our favor. Clearly, the record covers our markets in virtually every conceivable type of economic condition: booms, wars, recessions, inflation, and deflation. I guess it doesn't encompass a famine or a plague, and the period was one when the United States was a growing creditor nation to the world. It was also the era of The Cold War. Since we've slipped into debtor status and The Cold War appears to be on a meaningful wane, we'd better recognize that it is *possible* that circumstances will alter the future in such a way as to make this pattern irrelevant.

But this seems to me a very remote possibility. The strongest reason is the existence of the Federal Reserve Board, this nation's central bank. It's been in operation for some 75 years and is by far the most powerful force driving our economy.

It is primarily the Fed's actions, *both right and wrong*, that have made the markets behave as they have. Fed decisions about price inflation or deflation potential, wartime conditions, the economy's strength or weakness, and growth of the money stock have been the heavyweight forces in the economy. Sometimes Fed members have acted like a bull in a china shop, sometimes like a mouse in a church. But, withal, they've made the biggest decisions affecting our economic lives. Numerous studies and books have made this point abundantly clear, the latest major example of which is William Greider's *Secrets of The Temple: How the Federal Reserve Runs the Country*.

The Fed only has a few tools to work with in utilizing all its power. In fact, it can only (1) add or subtract money/credit from the banking system, (2) make that money multiply more or less rapidly, and (3) induce banks to borrow more or less from the system or each other. These tools basically haven't changed in 75 years, and if they do in the future we'll certainly be advised well in advance since they're controlled by law.

The interesting fact about each of these tools is that they must be put to use in, or they directly affect the short-term money market of, T-bills, certificates of deposit (CDs), federal funds, and such.

If the Fed wants to add money to the banking system, it buys Treasury paper, such as bills and notes, from its 32 primary dealers and credits their bank accounts in payment.

If the Fed wants to have that money go further in the banks, it reduces the reserves that the banks must keep behind their deposits.

Or the Fed can change its discount rate, the rate at which member banks borrow from the Fed system directly, and push the short-term interest rates in the direction of the change. It can also change margin requirements for stocks, and it almost daily carries out operations for its foreign central bank or other "customers" to influence the trend in those rates.

The bottom line is that each Fed action affects short-term interest rates to some degree.

Until the Fed's enabling law is changed, it's thus virtually certain this cause and effect relationship between Fed action and short-term rates will exist. And the markets we're interested in react to that relationship.

It's also useful to remember the homily stated by former Federal Reserve Board Chairman (1951–1970) William McChesney Martin, "The Federal Reserve's job is to take away the punch bowl just when the party gets going." The Fed is anticipatory and active in pursuing that goal.

This brings us to the critical point. Since the three markets in which we'll invest are markets *other* than the money market for short-term interest rates, we must know the connection between those rates and each of our other three markets. It's different for each.

With bonds, it is a direct, arithmetical connection, of course. Long-term bond yields are directly changed by any significant Fed action—even anticipated or perceived ones—on short-term rates. Bonds can and do move without Fed action, to be sure. But they always move with any important Fed action.

A rising trend in short-term rates pushes long-term rates up and, thereby, bond prices down. And vice versa. The formula is: yield equals coupon interest divided by price, period.

As we'll see in more detail in the chapter on stocks, the same pressure is true for the overall stock market. But, the connection is not directly to stock *prices*, but rather to stock *value*—what stocks should be worth. So the link between Fed action on short rates and stock prices is indirect. The stock market must perceive the value change before prices change. It often takes its time in doing this. Sooner or later, though, once the market believes the Fed is serious in its action, stock prices react in the same way as bond prices, *inversely* to the direction of short-term interest rates.

The best example of this came in 1987. The Fed got serious about forcing interest rates higher in April–May. The stock market didn't get the message until August, when it peaked. The Fed didn't quit, and the Crash was in major part caused by the reality of Fed action and the inflated stock prices that had been ignoring it.

Clearly, we now have the connection between the money market and the direction two of our three markets will take whenever the Fed acts.

What about gold?

Here, the linkage is looser. We do know that increases in inflation rates are positive for gold and decreases are negative. Gold is a fixed asset and prices of those assets tend to rise during inflation rate increases. They become more valuable than promises to pay fixed numbers of dollars in the future. This was certainly clear during the 1970s inflation binge, and the reverse held during the early 80s deflationary pressures.

Gold is also affected—and was especially so during the 1980s—by the movement of the dollar abroad. The relationship is inverse: A rising dollar equates with a falling gold price and vice versa. And since U.S. interest rates affect the attractiveness of the dollar to foreigners, as well as the domestic inflation rate, there is a connection between short-term interest rate trends here and gold prices. But as with stocks, the interaction is indirect. The market must get the message first.

In sum, then, as the legally endowed force that they are, Fed actions (1) directly affect bond prices, (2) indirectly affect stock prices, and (3) indirectly affect inflation pressures and, more loosely, the gold price.

These are quite sufficient reasons to believe that Fed action, as revealed in the only market in which it can be—the money market of short-term interest rates—will be a most powerful element in any future trends in our three markets. Note that this fact dovetails nicely with Fed-watching as a solution to our "whistling lemon" problem.

THOSE GAPS

Let's now address FRB actions in more practical terms. Specifically, just *how* causal is Fed action in creating bull and bear markets? The quickest way to answer this is to focus on the gaps in the every-calendar-year bull markets that we've identified. By gaps, I mean the *intra-year* non-bull market periods of the past four decades, and the slightly longer breaks bracketing World War II. We need to determine if there is any Fed-directed combination of inflation and interest rate trends that would prompt downtrends in all three of our markets simultaneously. If there is, we'll have strong evidence that gaps in our bull markets occur by Fed intent. If they do, we should be able to spot and prepare for them.

Theory says that *declining* inflation, coupled with *rising* interest rates should cause all three markets to react negatively. The disinflation pressures will tend to shove gold prices lower, and the rising rates do the same for bond and stock prices.

What about reality?

The record confirms that the Fed does not simply abdicate its responsibilities and allow rates to rise during declining inflation by acts of omission. It may act incorrectly by overdoing a given action, but it doesn't just sit on a policy forever. Look at the changing trends in T-bill rates that the Fed influences shown by Figure 2–1. That's not a "do-nothing" track. The rates are in constant flux, and we know most of that movement comes from *Fed action*. And that's fine for us. It doesn't matter whether the Fed acts correctly. We only need to know that it is acting, and *what* that action is.

In our previous summary of bull markets we saw that there have been four breaks in *continuous* bull markets among our three since World War II. Note that I'm talking here about *any* break where *all three* markets were in bear modes. This does not invalidate the "every year" bull market statement. Clearly, a break that occurs *within* a year doesn't disqualify that year as a bull market year. All the breaks since 1948 fit this description.

Now our question is, did inflation decrease in connection with all those breaks? And, did short-term interest rates rise during each of those periods? The previous tables and Figures 2–1 and 2–2 tell the story.

FIGURE 2-1
3-Month Treasury Bill Rate

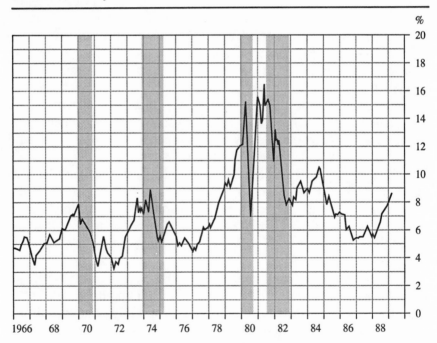

Monthly averages of daily closing yields. Yields are quoted on a bank-discount basis. Recession periods are shaded. Graph is based on data through March 1989.[*]

[*]Source: Courtesy of *The Business Picture*; Gilman Research, P. O. Box 20567, Oakland, CA 94620.

FIGURE 2-2
CPI with 12-Month Moving Average, 1954-1988 (monthly rate of change)*

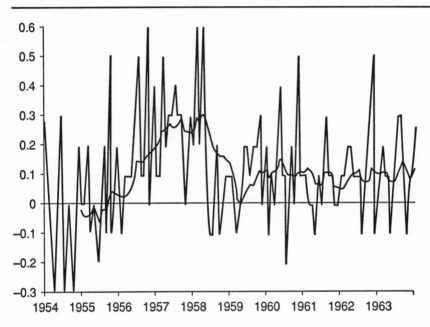

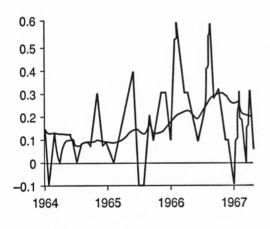

* Source: Kinsman and Associates

FIGURE 2–2—Continued

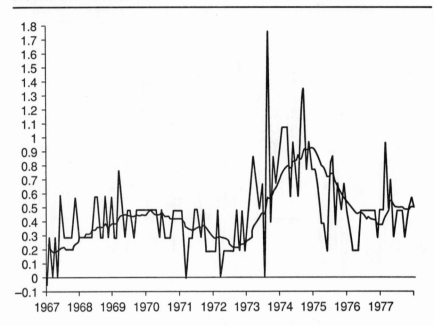

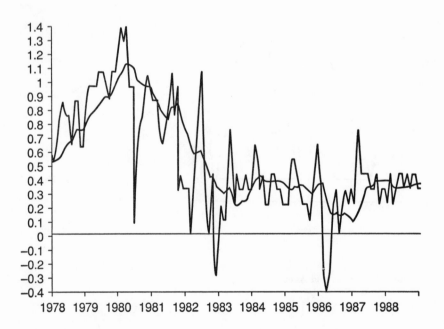

Not shown in Figure 2–2 is a rise in the inflation rate that occurred immediately after World War II. It quickly ran out of steam as the Fed began, during June 1946, to force short-term rates to *double* in two years. From that month's average yield (not shown in Figure 2–1) of 0.75 percent on four- to six-month prime commercial paper (where it had been pegged for two years), it jumped to 1.56 percent by October 1949. A recession began in 1946 and the Wholesale Price Index (now the Producer Price Index) then fell during 1948 and 1948. And, the longest post-war bull market gap took place from May 1946 to November 1948. The rate-rise/inflation-drop criteria were met.

The next bull market gap did not occur until March 1969, with a decline in the gold mining stocks joining the drops already underway in the general stock market and bonds. It lasted through December 1969.

Short-term interest rates had begun their rise in July 1967, but were to continue their ascent until January of 1970 before impacting the Customer Price Index (CPI) inflation rate, which then began a long descent until late 1972.

Again the pattern repeats itself, although this time the bull market break began well before the final turn in the inflation rate. However, 1970 was also a recession year, and it was undoubtedly the effects of that event that the markets anticipated.

At this point it should be noted that while the rising-interest-rate/declining-inflation pattern does occur around the beginning of each bull market gap, the timing of the interaction between the pattern and gap is variable. We cannot say this pattern always occurs *before* market breaks.

Nevertheless, the evidence is clearly developing that a sequence does exist. The Fed's action in forcing up short-term interest rates has *preceded* or coincided with both of our bull market gaps. And inflation rate declines have followed the start of the interest rate rises.

The next sequential gap rolled around from August through December 1974, this time in conjunction with a recession that followed a burst of inflation and the Fed's sharp upward shove on interest rates starting in early 1972. The markets did their predictable things, with bonds still in their long bear market, followed by a top in stocks in January 1973 and a decline in gold stocks in August 1974. Note the steep drop in the CPI from '75 to '77. That was definitely a Fed overkill, but the "right" combination for a bull market gap.

The next gap we have recorded came in late 1980. This was also a recession year preceded by sharply rising interest rates with a still high level of inflation. But price increases receded throughout the year under the relentless interest rate–recession pressure. The three markets all tanked, then recovered by late summer, only to dive again by the turn of the year 1981. Our pattern still holds, this time through the longest gap since 1946–48, some 11 months.

The last *apparent* gap in continuous postwar bull markets developed in late 1987 as the gold mining stocks peaked in November, following the earlier collapse of stocks and bonds. Ushering all this in, as usual, was a rise in short-term interest rates from September 1986, one that got serious in spring 1987. A CPI disinflation also got underway in late 1987.

From November 1987 until June 1, 1989, we could not be certain whether a gap truly existed or not. We had to await the stock and bond market rallies to discover if they'd meet our 25 percent critierion. The rallies started in August 1987 for monthly average bond prices and December 1987 for stocks.

By June 1989 we knew stocks had made it. The May 1989 average price for the Dow showed more than a 25 percent gain from its December 1987 average low by 52 points. There was an immediate bull market start following the '87 Crash, a historic first in timing. The "gap" was just one month in length.

To sum up, each of our bull market gaps occurred during a recession year, (except in 1988), and each one was preceded by an inflation problem that the Fed believed it must cool by forcing short-term interest rates higher. Declining inflation followed each rate rise. The record matches the theory.

Looking at the sequence of Fed action versus interest rate, inflation, and market reactions, we see that the monetary tightening always came first. But not every rising rate period (e.g., 1959–60) produced a bull market gap. In fact, gaps in all three markets occurred in only about *one-half* the tight money periods since 1946. Clearly, bull market gaps do not always follow rising rates.

What we can now conclude from the record is that (1) the Fed causes short-term interest rates to rise by policy decisions; (2) these rate rises have a propensity to create bull market gaps, but not always; still, (3) no bull market gap occurred since World War II that was *not* preceded by rising short-term interest rates; and (4) each previous gap was associated with an economic recession. (The jury's still out on any post-'87 recession.)

Therefore, it appears that Fed tightening of monetary conditions is a *critical step* in creating bull market gaps, and is certainly a condition to be watched carefully. Note also that *some* market declines did develop each time the Fed forced short-term rates to rise. But either the timing of each market's decline did not coincide sufficiently to generate a triple market gap, or the magnitude of the declines did not meet our tough criterion of greater than 20 percent for bear markets.

There's more here to study, but I'm getting ahead of my story. We'll come back to these conditions when I refine them for practical investing by introducing real-time indicators for each of our three markets.

One final, intriguing point about these gap periods leads to confidence that they should be brief. Each bull market gap prior to '87 occurred in association with a recession. Since it is well known that rising interest rates will produce an economic downturn *if* the condition lasts sufficiently long and/or the rate rise is sufficiently steep, a recession can be avoided if the Fed reverses the rate trend in time. Perhaps its members learned how to swing this by the late 1980s. They certainly hadn't before.

It also appears that if a bull market gap is to occur, it is invariably because the Fed acts so strongly that it slows the economy sharply while dampening inflation. But we can assume that the Fed will do everything possible to prevent the economy from slumping into another Depression. The political and human risks in that are simply too great, and the Humphrey-Hawkins Full Employment Act adds legal pressure. The result seems clearly to be that economic downturns become relatively brief and the markets' sequential bear turns are even briefer.

We can logically assume this process will continue in the future, until and unless the economic slump following a Fed tightening somehow gets totally out of hand. Past results don't create a future certainty on this point, to be sure, but the Fed does have powerful stimulatory tools in cutting interest rates and influencing governmental actions. We have no evidence at this date that such actions will be inadequate.

True, there are reasons to be concerned about a runaway downturn in the future, especially with the enormous personal, corporate, and public debt hanging over the economy of the late 1980s. But as Woody Allen quipped, "while it's said the lion and lamb will lie down together, that ain't the way to bet." At least not yet.

In summary, by understanding how the Fed acts and why, we can assume there are strong probabilities that a bull market in one of the three that I've focused on will be annual occurrences in the future, as in the past. Interruptions will happen, but the probability for their being brief is also high under any foreseeable political-economic climate in Washington.

What's more, we are tipped off to the possibility of a bull market gap by having clear evidence that the Fed is serious about pushing short-term interest rates higher.

Even after more than 25 years investment experience, I can say that this knowledge has made my advisory job much easier. It should do the same for your investing.

As we've addressed the first of this chapter's original three points, we can now concentrate on how to identify the bull markets early enough to profit from them in real time. And how to select the best vehicles to participate. That may seem like a tall order. It really isn't in the Right Market Method.

To approach the identification issue, we need to analyze what we should expect from real-world investing. Those bull market runs listed earlier in this chapter seem awfully tempting, but investing reality produces much more modest results, no matter what you've heard.

CHAPTER 3

WHAT TO EXPECT FROM A WINNING MARKET

The best way to double your money is to fold it over once and put it in your billfold.—"Kin" Hubbard

We constantly hear about the size of gains that investors can achieve. One newsletter promotion I received a few years ago touted over a 1600 percent return "every year." A friend who was starting a commodities trading firm several years ago told me with a straight face that he expected better than 30 percent *compound annual* returns for clients in that volatile business. The business is now defunct, although I don't know if that condition was caused by over promised returns. It's certainly suspect. In any case, the fact is that return hype is pervasive in the investment world, despite some regulation of it.

The problem is that some returns *can be* spectacular—for short runs. But real-time investing over the long run produces modest results, even for professionals. And investing is a long-term process. How often do people acquire funds to invest and then simply stop investing them? Truth is that the average person begins investing excess capital when disposable funds are first acquired, and only rarely ceases before death. I'd say that's "long run."

What kind of real returns are we talking about? When we discuss periods of a decade or more that cover both bull and bear markets in the historically most reliable gain-producing securities (common stocks) and if we don't begin our measurement at or near a market low for extra oomph, we're talking about a sound barrier in the range of 20–25 percent *compound* per year. And that's with nearly ideal picking of tops and bottoms. Over the long haul a more realistic goal for the average investor should be 12 percent to 15 percent compound per annum.

Before you think that's pretty low, consider that 12 percent compounded annually *doubles* capital in just *six years*. Most investors would love to have achieved that return over the long term. On top of that, the total return for common stocks from 1926 through 1988, *including dividends*, was 10.0 percent compounded annually.

Let's look at why 12 percent to 15 percent compounded is a realistic target.

The first question must be, shouldn't we always try to make as much as we can? It may surprise you to know the answer is: not necessarily. That can be dangerous to your wealth. The problem is the risk I just noted.

The truth is that investing for a return greater than that of virtually riskless Treasury bills involves taking increased risk, the amount of which depends on the investment itself. Whether you wish to take a given risk to potentially increase your return should be determined by your temperament, objectives, probably your age, and almost certainly how much capital you have compared to your future needs. In short, the how-much-to-try-to-make question is really a personal one, not a universal one.

Unfortunately, there is a presumption on Wall Street that doesn't want to bother with this caveat. It says that making the most money is always the best idea. Once that thought is imbedded in investors' minds they are far more inclined to transact to achieve greater returns. Of course, transactions are the life blood of the Street, yet they may be just a bloodletting for the investor.

This is also where the performance game enters the picture. It uses targets—usually a market average—to convince investors to strive for more: "Haven't beaten the Dow Industrials this quarter? Just shift to XYZ and UVW and that should do it next quarter."

The fact is that this is a very misleading idea. If you doubt this, ask yourself whether you, if you were an investor living entirely on investment income, should be bothered about how to achieve market-beating capital gains? (Other than possibly a few percent as an annual inflation hedge)? An average income investor may be taking risks equal to about *one-third* that of the S&P 500. Should that risk be *tripled* to match the market return when interest and dividends are all that are needed? Of course not. Nor should a large number of transactions be made in lower risk issues to achieve the same goal. Clearly, income investors are a major exception to playing the performance game. More on this shortly.

Now let's look at what history has to tell us about realistic returns.

THE RECORD

Long-term studies of market returns through good and bad times make it clear that expecting to earn even mid-teen percentage gains annually on a compound basis is not going to be an easy job. And achieving much over 20 percent per year on the same basis will be most unusual over time. Yes, those returns are possible for brief stretches in higher risk investments. But a ten-year, 25 percent compound annual return, for example (that's a 358.2 percent total return), is about as usual in the investment markets, any of them, as it is on the crap table. If the odds on any one try don't get you, the number of tries will. Here's the record.

Investment Returns, 1926–1988
(Compounded annually; %)

Common stocks	10.0
Government bonds	4.4
Treasury bills	3.5
Consumer Prices	3.1

Now, since these figures include the 1987 stock market Crash and bond bear market, it can be argued that they're deflated in those categories. But at the end of 1986 the 61-year stock return was also an even 10 percent per annum and the government bond return was the same 4.4 percent annually. Not much difference in the long-range scheme of things.

One could also argue that these numbers are diminished by the famous 1929 Crash, the Depression, and the 35-year bear market in bonds from 1946 to 1981. You can argue it, but you should recall the the Depression featured the second largest stock market *gain* of the century, and the whole period took in the great bull markets of the 50s, 60s, and 80s. And parts of this era, especially 1932–37 and 1981–87, showed a near doubling of bond prices. Besides, who's to say that the next 63 years will be markedly different from this 63?

One factor does make a difference: inflation. The 1971–1988 period, which includes the latest price boom and deflationary eras, raised the annual CPI average to 6.4 percent, the Treasury bill return to 7.6 percent, and Treasury bond return to 8.4 percent per year. But it hiked the common stock annual return by only one point to 11.0 percent.

These numbers are what investors are up against in broad market, historical terms. They represent the averages. But what about the maximum achievable market returns in great bull markets?

The investor who bought the S&P Composite Index at each stock market low and sold at the high—the ideal—in the 39 years through 1987 would have made a staggering 132 times the original stake. With dividends added at an assumed average compound rate of 4 percent per year over the periods that stocks were owned during this period (zero return assumed while out of the market), this ideal investor would have achieved a 24.1 percent compound annual return. That's the omniscient stock market investor taking exactly the market level of risk, owning the whole market at the best times in the greatest overall bullish era of the century. That's a rather substantial achievement to beat, wouldn't you say?

More recent research supports this return as a potential maximum, too. In his July 25, 1988 column in *Forbes*, newsletter performance tracker Mark Hulbert noted that the best-performing of any service he monitored since July 1, 1980, *The Zweig Forecast*, achieved a compound return of 21.7 percent per year through mid-1988. That service's risk level averaged modestly above that of the S&P 500. True, this was in a shorter period than the full postwar era noted above, and it included bonds and leverage. But several other studies show similar caps on money manager returns over decade-long periods in stock bull markets.[1] So, depending on the period studied, a 21 to 24 percent compound annual return on stocks has more than modest support as a modern performance hurdle when taking risk in a stock portfolio at about the risk level of the overall market. And 10 percent per annum is the very long-term stock return. (Figures include dividends.)

There's a Grand Canyon gap between the two extremes. Of course, they arise from totally different philosophies of trading, but we're looking for maximum realistic returns at this point, not at the merit of various strategies.

Let's dig further into that gap. The stock market indicators I've developed and used for most of the past decade (detailed in Chapter 6) provide an interesting comparison. They've been tracked back to January 1967, in part to provide a tough period in which to perform, since the start was near a market high and the finish at December 1988 was only moderately above a market low.

The *buy-hold* annual compound rate for the S&P 500, since January '67, using average monthly prices, was 5.8 percent *without* dividends. The RMM stock-only indicators achieved 8.6 percent on the same basis, or *nearly-half again* as much. Both are back-tested real-world results during multiple bull and bear markets. Add in dividends at an assumed 4 percent annual compound rate during time invested, and the returns are 9.8 percent and 12.6 percent, respectively. (Note the buy-hold returns' proximity to the historical stock return.)

The returns seem startlingly modest, don't they? Less than half that hurdle rate. Well, it was a tough era, all right. More importantly, out of the 22-year period, the RMM indicators' signaled return suffered from being invested in stocks only 9.5 years, or 43 percent of the time. No return was assigned to the 57 percent of the time that was out of stocks. RMM was

---

[1] See *Small Stocks Big Profits*, by Gerald Perritt, Dow Jones-Irwin, 1988; and *The New Contrarian Investment Strategy*, by David Dreman, Random House, 1982. Further explanation is in the Appendix.

in gold and bonds most of the other 12.5 years. The buy-hold strategy was, of course, invested all the time.

Clearly, this is one of RMM's great advantages. It provides alternate bull market choices, so the bull market invested time increases. In this case it rises to 19.8 of the 22 years if we use all three markets' signals from 1967 through 1988.

Its return? If one had bought each of the bull markets and sold it as signaled in the Composite Record in Figure 10–1 (Chapter Ten), the combined annual compound return would have been 15.2 percent. This figure assumes compounding of gains in each market and the simple addition of gains in one market to those in the others. It *excludes* dividends and interest, and latter of which would have added over 180 percent to bond market results alone.

On the other hand, RMM did include gold bullion during its greatest bull market of the century, which gave it a moonshot assist. Yet that is exactly what the Right Market approach is designed to do: identify the great bull markets in any phase of the inflation-deflation cycle.

This is also the reason that the RMM includes a deflation hedge—long-term government bonds—among its alternatives, even though they provided little help during this particular period.

CONCLUSIONS

Evidence suggests that the U.S. securities providing the best returns over the past 20 to 40 years, common stocks, have had an *optimum* achievable compound return somewhere modestly in excess of 20–22 percent per year in the averages. This also implies that although long historical returns *average* around 10 percent on the same basis, some market strategies can do better than that in bull market eras and in multiple bull/bear periods. But returns will tend to gravitate toward the historical record, and a *realistic target* return will be only moderately in excess of that historical figure. About 12–15 percent per year compounded seems an achievable target. This is just below the back-tested return RMM achieved over the past 22 years.

BEATING THE MARKET

We've been discussing performance, without emphasizing the word, as a means to the end of determining a realistic target return for risk taken. Now we have one for moderate-risk investors. All those claims you hear about returns of hundreds of percent over a *short* time frame are very likely not to be replicable in the next time frame, or to require substantially higher risk (statistically as much as 30 times the risk of the S&P 500, as is common in futures contracts).

But what about the frequently heard cry in the financial media and among the professional money manager tracking firms that "beating the market" is the name of the game? Is it? Or if it is, should it be?

My answer is emphatically "no" to both questions, except under very limited conditions: (1) for anyone who chooses to accept relatively high statistical risk investing, including futures, options, and volatile stocks; (2) with managed assets whose manager has set a goal that includes "beating the market"; or (3) for managers and other investors where the period covered is sufficiently long-term to include at least one complete bull and bear cycle.

Why these? Investors fitting the first criterion should be prepared to live by the sword, and presumably, to die by it. The sword can include market comparisons, although they're often meaningless in high-volatility markets. Then the management crowd needs as much fairness as any type investor, and statistically a full bull/bear cycle should provide it. Otherwise, emphasizing short-term performance merely promotes short-term trading in a field that is long-term by nature.

Are there any reasons long-term investors should be subjected to the short-term performance game? We've already noted a significant exception: income investors. One possible reason might be that some advisors/managers could get by with hand-sitting or large dollops of poor judgment if their results weren't measured. Fine, measure their results, but do so in a way that counts the *goals* of *both* the managers and the clients. Don't shove performance down their throats without clearly identifying what they are attempting to do.

That only plays into Wall Street's hands for more transactions. And that often produces poorer results before better.

Of course, this concentration on short-term performance is truly a function of our impatience. It is the "whistling lemon" come home to squeeze, as it were. This suggests we're probably stuck with it. But we can make it fairer.

The fact is that numerous studies have been made of "beating the market" efforts.[1] Results have shown that over periods of 7 to 10 years, where bull/bear cycles are complete, the difference between the average money manager's performance and a market return is on the order of the cost of fees and transactions. Remember that a market index doesn't have to pay commissions, management fees, or other expenses. Plus, the index changes direction at will, while mere mortals have to figure whether the turn is meaningful or not.

One can argue that a money manager or advisor *should* be sufficiently expert before hanging out his or her shingle to be able to exceed market returns in order to cover those fees. This begs the question. We can still ask, for whom is this important? Not for income investors. And what about the investing public that is averse to even market-level risks, such as many successful middle-age people? That's a large group: in terms of age, soon to be America's largest demographic segment. These are the people who say, as Will Rogers was reported to have, "I'm not so interested in the return *on* my money as the return *of* my money." Why should those who agree try to beat the market or hire an advisor who tries hard to do so?

In fact, trying *not* to "beat the market" has caught on dramatically. Using a market *index* as a control on investment returns has been so successfully propounded to financial institutions by market theoreticians that a very large amount of money is now being professionally managed via index funds.

Pensions and Investment Age, a respected publication in the professional money management field, keeps a running tab on the 30 largest index fund managers and the money they have under their wings. Since the index movement got rolling in the late 1970s, the totals of money indexed to the market (e.g., to the S&P 500) have exploded. In November 1980, the

publication estimated that some $9 billion of managed money
was indexed. By that month in 1983 the number was $37.5 bil-
lion, and by November 1987 it had swelled to $145 billion, a
16-fold increase in seven years. Clearly, indexing has arrived
in capital management. We must also note that this still represents less than 5 percent of the $3.035 trillion estimated to be
under management in the United States at the end of 1987.

The conclusion must be that a good deal of sophisticated
money, albeit still not the majority of it, has agreed with the
idea that it makes little sense to attempt beating the market.
Since our realistic target returns are in the range of long-term
market returns, I believe indexing is a wise alternative to playing the performance game.

There's another factor at work here: the *balance* side of
the equation. We've noted that T-bills are considered virtually
riskless, stock averages have a moderate risk level, and gold
mining stocks in particular carry approximately twice as much
risk as the S&P 500 Index. It's important to understand how
this is measured. We don't need to get into great detail, as this
subject can become very technical. (For those who wish such
a discussion, see "Risk Levels of Actively Traded Securities,"
published by Kinsman Associates, Inc., 1987.)

Figure 3–1 graphically shows three levels of risk as measured in securities. Figure 3–1(a) represents a T-bill or guaranteed time deposit: a fixed return, growing in value over time.
Figure 3(b) exemplifies a moderate risk vehicle, where prices
fluctuate around a growth trend (which is unknown at the out-
set), but only to a moderate degree. An element of uncertainty
is present, not only as to the growth trend slope, but whether
the next very short move will be up or down. Figure 3–1(c)
shows a volatile investment, with far more pronounced price
fluctuations and uncertainty.

The measurement of securities risk is simply a calculation
of how far and fast the price deviates from its growth trend.
So what we're really measuring is volatility, which mathemati-
cians term *variability*, and that's why the terms *risk, variability*,
and *volatility* are used interchangeably in securities parlance.

At this point, all that we need recognize is that if we combine all three of these graphs, *equally weighted* in a portfolio,

FIGURE 3–1
Risk and Return Variability

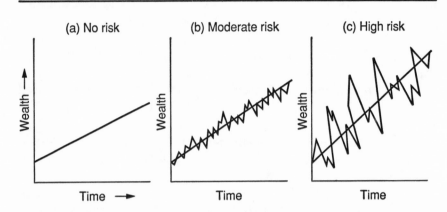

the portfolio's volatility would tend toward the center of the three. We could also tip the *balance* toward the risky end by overweighting in the most volatile portion, and toward the no-risk end by overweighting with that segment.

This set of facts has a significant implication. Performance is not only greatly affected by risk taken, in that assuming high risk in rising markets should generate excess return and doing so in falling markets will achieve excess losses, but performance is also affected by the *type* of security chosen and the *amount* of it. Hold excess T-bills or short maturity T-notes during a rising stock market and you underperform. Do the same in a falling market—the correct action—and you may achieve smaller loss-es, but probably not gains, unless you're close to 100 percent invested in the Treasuries.

Achieving all of this may not be too much to ask of a money manager who is managing for optimum growth. But what about those who are managing for clients whose stated objective is preservation of capital with *modest* growth on top of it? What has "the market" got to do with that?

Clearly this is important to our target return discussion. Achieving modestly greater returns than the market over long time frames is what we're suggesting. But accomplishing that will almost certainly require, in my experience, many short periods of underperformance along with some market-beating times.

This brings up a last angle to the risk versus performance matter. It's critical to our approach to investing. Since risk can be controlled and adjusted by changing the portfolio mix as well as by market timing, someone with a sound bull market identification procedure should take advantage of it to increase volatility of holdings during clear bull markets and reduce volatility at other times due to increased market risks. This may indeed cause the underperformance referred to above when compared to the market during periods when the markets don't respond to their identified risks, but it still achieves prescribed objectives over the longer term. (To do so, it should also generate returns in excess of the markets at times.)

The year 1987 was a fine case in point. RMM indicators triggered stock market sales as early as May, causing portfolios based on it to underperform in both the second and third quarters that year. But it was not only the clearly correct strategy, as the October Crash proved, but it did not interrupt the 12 percent–plus compound annual return RMM achieved over multiple years.

Thus, a portfolio that targets top-notch performance must deal successfully with these key elements: (1) good selection of growth vehicles, (2) assumption of volatility in them that exceeds market levels, (3) accurate timing of buys and sells, and (4) holding of cash equivalents only when major market downturns are about to occur. Or, a star performer must excel sufficiently in selection or timing to offset any negatives in the volatility and cash balance factors. These combinations are certainly achievable by skilled investors. But the investor who wishes not to take greater than market risk in individual issues and who simply wants to hold a modest amount of cash at all times starts with two of four strikes against him.

To see the effect of just the cash holding, a common step for risk-averse investors, consider how a cash position of 20 percent of portfolio affects results even in a relatively high interest rate period. Let's assume the performance target is the Dow Industrials, which gained 20 percent in a 12-month period, during which 8 percent was earned on T-bills in which the cash was held. The bills delivered a net interest return of 1.6 percent on the cash portion. The other 80 percent of portfolio must now earn 18.4 percent just to bring the portfolio up to our Dow's return. Thus, that segment's annual return rate must be 23 percent (18.4 divided by 0.8). That's doable, of course, but it requires either a volatility assumption of 15 percent more than the Dow or sufficiently better timing than the Dow to outgain it by 15 percent. Either or both of these assumptions may be unacceptable to the risk-averse investor, especially over long-range time frames. Those who expect market-beating results every year should at least acknowledge the irrelevance of it for risk-averse and income investors.

SUMMARY

We've now developed three critical points about making money with the Right Market Method.

1. The amount you wish to target as an annual or multi-year return is a personal decision based on *your* needs and risk tolerance. Increasing returns usually requires assuming greater risk. Not all investors wish to, or need to, do either (e.g., the pure-income or the risk-averse investor).

2. Achieving returns that, over time, approach the 15 percent annual compound level or more, actually requires success with four management criteria:

- Correct issue selection for growth.
- Risk in excess of market level for each growth issue, or
- Good market timing, or both.
- Sufficient balance among growth issues and any cash or equivalents held to optimize portfolio growth.

Since elevated risk and growth are uncomfortable or unnecessary concepts for many investors, the performance game regrettably ignores a large segment of the investing public.

3. Return is constrained on the upside by the fact that investing is a long-term occupation, no matter how short one's trading horizon is. That appears to have produced practical limits on achievable returns. For the broad list of common stocks in multiple bull/bear time frames, a realistic target return with average risk, including dividends, appears to be in the area of 12 to 15 percent per year compounded.

We've also seen that our Right Market Method, using real-time indicators and assuming somewhat more than S&P 500 Index risk, has produced long-term returns significantly above that of the S&P alone.

There's a final point. Since the RMM is a long-term investing approach, an over-emphasis on achieving much higher than historical returns will lead to impatience and usually to increased market trading. Impatience is the worst enemy of this method. Active trading may easily lead to underperforming our approach because of costs.

Now we can turn our attention to the second aspect of our framework, how to analyze the markets, both from a macro- or broad-based approach and from an individual indicator selection standpoint.

CHAPTER 4

USING THE RIGHT
MARKET METHOD

---

*If some people got their rights they would complain of being
deprived of their wrongs.—Oliver Hexford*

The word "right" in the Right Market Method has, of course,
nothing to do with rights, or with the political right wing. It
simply means correct. But, if RMM is to be correct for investors,
there must be a practical way of using it. Naturally there is,
and it begins with a correct overview of each market.

MARKETS FIRST

Let's check a few basics. Each of our three markets can be
seen as a single entity, as, essentially, a monolith. Each is
measured by one or more indexes of the whole market, and
more importantly, we can invest in any of those measures. We
can literally own each market.

Among the multiple index forms for each market are
futures contracts for Treasury bonds and notes and for municipal bonds. Gold has futures for various bullion sizes, the most
popular of which are the 100 ounce contracts. In stocks we have
futures for the S&P 500, S&P 100, Major Market Index, and the
like.

Then there are the proxies for the index forms: stock index
mutual funds, gold bullion coins in numerous denominations,
and bullion itself; Treasury bond mutual funds plus short- and
medium-term bond funds for all categories from Treasuries to
corporates to municipals. Not all are pure plays on each market,

but enough are to say that we now truly have wide choices in how to fully "play" each of our markets.

The importance of this single entity concept is that we are not required to look at each market piecemeal—by individual stock or by industry, for example, nor by specific bond or each issuer of gold bars or coins. We can if we wish to do so, but we can focus on "the market" if we wish, as well.

This means we can take a "top down" approach to our markets by identifying a whole market's trend and then either investing directly in a broad vehicle for it, or going a step further and looking at specific narrow vehicles like individual stocks and bonds.

This choice is an advantage that all too few investors use, in my experience. Most spend a great deal of time and money focusing on the segments or individual issues and not the over-all markets. In fact, this was how I was taught to approach stocks nearly 30 years ago, before the advent of stock index contracts and index mutual funds, let alone gold or bond futures.

Maybe the "issue pickers" bother little with overall market trends because they don't want to invest in indexes or options on them and therefore ignore or downplay the big picture to get to the narrow one. Maybe it's because they believe the rewards are greater in individual issues. In recent years this has increasingly struck me as an odd way to invest. It's far easier to determine an overall market trend than it is to find specific winners within that market. And the market's trend accounts for a large a part of the average price action of its individual components. RMM starts top down and gets to individual issue selection second.

Maybe many investors have become so accustomed to dealing with bull markets for the past 20 years—at least in stocks and gold, since bear markets in them have been very brief compared to bull trends—that they're assuming the bull will bail out errors soon enough. They should remember or study 1973–74.

For argument's sake, let's look at how the gold and bond markets function as monoliths.

With gold, every form of gold bullion, including bullion coins, moves with the gold price. It may be that Comex futures determine the gold price while that exchange is open, rather than the London price fixing or New York dealers' spot prices, or it may be the latter two. But a gold price change of significance, wherever it originates, pushes all cash and futures gold prices in the same direction. The size of the price move will vary by segment, but direction rarely does. What's more, decent price changes usually take the gold mining stocks with them, although as we'll see, the mining stocks often have a life of their own. The gold market, therefore, is nearly monolithic in practice, even though it has numerous segments to invest in.

The bond market is even more uniform. Whether Treasury, corporate, or municipal issues, any real move in the long maturity end of the market pushes all long bonds the same direction. It's only in the varying maturities that direction discrepancies occur. Short-term bonds can react differently from long. Although, even here, if the long-end movement is significant, say ½ to ¾ point price change, it's rare that all maturity segments don't move in the same direction. Again, it is usually only the magnitude of the change that differs, and this is also true of corporate, municipal, and Treasury markets at the same time.

Even in the stock market we have a strong monolithic tendency, although it's fair to say that it's less pervasive than with either gold or bonds. Historical studies of stock price movements have discovered that something on the order of 60 percent of the average stock's price movement over time occurs because of the *overall* market's moves. Far less of the average price change comes from developments with the individual stock itself.

This is not to say that it's not worth selecting individual stocks. These figures are averages, with all the foibles they bring. And finding individual stock winners can be far more rewarding *per occurrence* than discovering a correct market trend. But, over time, this differential tends to disappear as losers offset gainers.

So, a key point about our Right Market Method is its top down approach. It focuses on the market first due to the markets' importance in the price movement of individual issues within it.

Having said this, note that once the overall trend is recognized RMM is then extendable into individual issue selection, either through its own risk guidelines, or by use of any other issue selection methods.

In short, RMM gets the market horse out front, steers you toward advantageous vehicles, and is compatible with any additional issue selection approach, if you wish to use one.

THE INDICATOR MAZE

In the introduction we noted the simple secret behind our indicator-based Right Market Method: the price inflation-deflation process. Prices, at whatever level they're measured, can clearly only rise, remain constant, or fall. And fortunately, there is one financial market that reacts best to each of those price trends, as we've seen. Let's now refine this.

Prices, while rising for example, can either accelerate or decelerate. That is, the *rate* of rise can speed up or slow down, while still rising. This is elemental.

This distinction is often confused, however. Take the word inflation. Inflation means rising prices, usually at the consumer level. It says nothing about the rate of rise. So, a price rise of 6 percent per year is inflation, and so are 8 percent and 3 percent and so on.

If prices change from a 6 percent annual rate of increase to an 8 percent rate, however, inflation is accelerating. And it is this condition, the acceleration, that is most troublesome to the financial markets. It is not the simple fact that prices are rising. Consumer prices have been rising, with only two real exceptions, ever since the Second World War. We've still had eight up/down stock market cycles. One way or another, accelerating inflation played a part in each bear move.

Given this fact, we must be most concerned about the acceleration or deceleration of prices, not just whether prices are rising or falling. This adds a complication to our simple secret, because price direction is far easier to determine than the changes in rate within a given direction. True, each government price report announces rate change as well as direction.

But the key question the markets ask goes still further: Is the new rate of change in a *sustainable* trend? Will it continue, accelerate, or decelerate? This is what makes the job of selecting trend indicators much more difficult. We can't be content with indicators that show the trend, up or down, or even those that reveal whether the current trend is accelerating or decelerating. We require indicators that identify *sustainable* accelerations and decelerations in prices. And what's more, these same indicators must catch trend changes that the markets will react to. No use in catching trend changes if the markets don't think they're real.

Fortunately, the markets are highly sensitive to inflation trend changes and are quite efficient. Fact is, if we get the real inflation trend change right, the markets will come around to realizing it relatively sooner than later. We're on solid ground if we can discover true trend changes and relate to them to each market's potential. This is the basis we'll use in selecting our inflation indicators.

Inflation price indicators are indeed basic to our bull market identification, but they are hardly the whole story. In truth, they're only one of five types of indicators which many students of the markets believe are most important. These five, taken somewhat out of order of importance for ease in picking an acronym out of them, are sentiment, interest rates, market momentum, prices (consumer), and (in an advisory sense) low risk for market conditions.

These form the SIMPL system:

Sentiment
Interest rates
Market momentum
Prices (consumer)
Low risk for market

WHY USE MARKET INDICATORS AT ALL?

Before looking at the *raison d'être* for each type, we should be reminded why market indicators are needed. After all, to many investors they are too technical and just complicate the buy-sell process.

Aside from the fact that in our whistling lemon world such complications are a way of life and must be dealt with, valid market indicators are needed for several practical reasons. The first is to eliminate the worst enemies of investing: fear and greed.

It's probably safe to say that more money has been lost or just not made because of those two emotions than any other. Fear, because it paralyzes rational thought and prevents taking action at critical junctures. It's why the market bromide, "the market climbs a wall of worry" is the cliché that it is. The bull market takeoff in August 1982 amidst the worst international debt crisis since the 1920s is a splendid example of this point. Fear was exactly what that market fed on because the economic facts, Federal Reserve Board resolve, and many technical indicators ran totally contrary to the reasons for fear. The fearful missed out. (RMM didn't.)

Greed is just as dangerous, although it was certainly taken to new heights by many during the 1982–87 bull run, especially in the takeover games. Probably more than any other emotion is was a key to the 1987 Crash. It certainly wasn't rationality that carried stocks to the extreme overvaluations of August 1987. And greed played a key role keeping that bull market alive. It took longer to die after reaching excess valuations than any in recent memory. In fact, the nearest equivalent was the 1962–68 run. But again, economic facts, Fed determination, and numerous technical indicators warned of both bulls' demise, even though it can be argued that the 80s bull merely stopped to graze before charging off in 1988–89. (RMM caught both the "graze" and re-charge periods.)

Valid market indicators do more than eliminate fear and greed. In helping to accomplish that big task they bring to bear a *discipline* that is highly useful for other reasons. Knowing when and how much to invest in any market is just as important in periods when fear or greed aren't rampant as when they are.

The 1983–84 interim stock market top was, in hindsight, one that could have been ignored. The correction of 1984 lasted less than 8 months and measured about 20 percent in the averages. But the elements that went into the peak formation— from economic conditions to market technical position—did not pre-ordain a brief stock fall. They were virtually identical to all major market tops in the past 40 years. The most astute investor could do little more than guess that a top of that sort would be followed by a brief and moderate correction. A sell was warranted by a discipline that protects against both large and small disasters. What's more, the same discipline should have caught the next bull swing at lower levels than it sold, thereby increasing profits more than a "hold through" approach would have. RMM did.

The third major value of using valid indicators is their ability to control what we could call "informed opinion" about market trends. By that I mean the opinions that most seasoned investors constantly tend to form about market action. The amount and complexity of economic and technical information constantly surrounding the markets is legion. Barely a minute goes by during a trading day, certainly not an hour, that some new piece of it isn't unveiled. From nearly 30 years experience with the markets, I can tell you that only a minute fraction of this is valid in determining true market trends over the medium term. Perhaps a larger percentage of it is important in very short-term market aberrations, but I don't use that approach so I can't confirm that. In any case, investors who follow markets closely enough can't help but be tempted to form trend opinions by some of this flood of data. It is simply so pervasive (as in watching Financial News Network, for example) and our desire to make both sense and money from it so great, that we can't help but wish to establish an informed opinion about some parts of it.

Human nature being what it is, I've never found anyone, including myself, who regularly came to correct decisions based on this steady informational diet alone. I think the markets are simply too complex to be correctly analyzed via this data flow. Instead, the most successful market professionals have established some form of filtering discipline that tells them which pieces of the data mountain are useful and which aren't.

That's exactly what RMM does, and it does so with such selectivity that an investor following it rarely needs to know anything happening in the markets or the economy more often than about once a week. Only occasionally, when the indicators are on alert, might it require two or three readings. Total time following our indicators rarely should exceed an hour a week.

The final reason for using market indicators is that it is only through them that a multimarket, asset allocation concept such as RMM can function. It's a virtual certainty that if emotions, personal opinions, and the data flood make accurate buy-sell decisions difficult in one market, or even two, it nearly obviates them in three different markets at once. What's more, the asset allocation decisions of how much to invest in each market, are handled mechanically by RMM. To do this any other way would be chaotic.

In sum, valid market indicators play a critical role in developing correct decisions about our complex markets, be they through emotion or opinion control or in calling attention to historically important market/economic or technical conditions. The Right Market Method then goes a step further and organizes these indicators into a useful methodology. That's the SIMPL approach.

INDICATOR CATEGORIES

The next question must be, why use these particular indicator types?

The short answer is that market theory requires using at least those in the SIMPL acronym. In fact, many more could be utilized to forecast market trends, and numerous advisors and investors do so. My studies have shown that these are not only the most important indicator types, but they are fully applicable to each market, and they are sufficient in themselves as trend callers. We don't need to use more, except perhaps in short-term buy-sell timing. The four categories in SIMP are enough for our medium-term RMM approach, as history has shown. ("L" is a risk reminder, not an indicator.)

Sentiment represents the critical market element of psychology. Every investor knows that's one of the major forces in any market movement. It doesn't matter which market we choose, psychology is there. How many times have you watched a market roar off or collapse without any specific news? Pundits usually term it a "technical move." Chances are it's just psychology crowding around a given idea, although these days that's often linked with nonpsychological program trading. Whatever, no serious investor doubts that market psychology is highly important to trend development, albeit often a short-term phenomenon, not long-term.

The real question with psychology is how to gauge it, not whether it's important. My studies have found a sound quantitative measure called the *Bullish Consensus*, published by Market Vane of Pasadena, California. It's available daily for each of our three markets and is based on polls of futures traders' sentiment. It has the added advantage of bringing futures market opinion to bear on the cash markets we will use. As we turn the corner into the 1990s, that is a critical plus for our approach. Details of use of this sentiment yardstick are discussed in the respective market chapters, as are each of the other specific indicators within the SIMPL system.

Incidentally, there are other measures of sentiment that may be helpful. The oldest, and certainly a well-respected service, comes from *Investors Intelligence*, published by Chartcraft, Inc. of New Rochelle, New York. It measures advisors' bullishness and bearishness.

Another of our indicators I've called market momentum, although the term *momentum* has a specific meaning in market technicians' parlance different from the one I'm using here. My use is to designate market trend and relative staying power of the trend based on how the market is moving relative to its recent past movement. This makes use of a simple moving average (MA) for each market, based on a key index of that market. As indexes, we primarily use the Dow Industrials for stocks, the nearby Comex gold futures for gold, and the nearby Chicago Board of Trade (CBT) T-bond futures for long-term government bonds. I've found these to be the most readily available, both during the trading day and in the financial press anywhere in the country.

A market's position relative to a key moving average is most important in detecting whether the market is responding to events, information, or psychology in such a way as to change its recent trend. A well-tested MA acts both as a trend change detector, to be used in conjunction with other indicators, and as a basket to catch information that may have been missed by those other indicators.

As a reminder about figuring MAs, all you need do is add up the closing prices for whatever index or security you're using (e.g., the Dow Industrials) for the MA period, say 39 weeks. Then, divide by the number of dates (39), and plot this result under the final week's number. Next week, add the new closing price to the prior *total* and subtract the first price in the series from it. Again divide by 39 and plot the new number under the final week's close. The new series of numbers plotted is the moving average.

There is one problem with even the best MA, and it's a point to be wary of. Figure 4–1 illustrates both the advantages and flaw with MAs. In the 1982–86 chart note how well the widely used 39-week MA caught the Dow's major bull moves in 1982 and 1984–85, as well as the top in 1984. Clearly, it didn't nail the exact tops and bottoms by itself, but it came respectably close.

The second chart reveals the flaw. It shows neatly during the 1978–80 period when the MA caught trading range flip-flops just as readily as it did the start of major moves. Using an MA of a different length won't solve the problem either, because a shorter one will catch more false moves and a longer one will be unacceptably slow on the great moves.

The solution to this is one that too many investors (and several well-known advisors) ignore. Never use an MA alone to make buy-or-sell decisions. Always use it as either a confirmation of other indicator signals, or as one of a group of signals. But never let it make up your mind by itself.

In addition, it's usually wise to adapt a filter of a couple of percent both above and below the MA. Crossover signals then come with breaks above or below the *filter percent line*, not the exact MA level. This helps avoid the difficulty of too many investors following the same MA and creating a whipsaw action around it.

During the 1978–80 period mentioned above, if other indicators were correctly formulated and read, they should have revealed, as RMM did, that the proper elements for a sustained bull market in stocks were simply not in place, no matter what the MA did. This didn't mean the market had to plunge, but rather that opposing forces were in about equal balance in the market and that no mechanical MA was apt to give meaningful signals until something else changed.

With this important caveat to watch for, we should have no fear of using tested MAs in our SIMPL approach. Their whipsaw tendencies can be avoided.

The two other indicator types in our method, interest rates and consumer prices, are true fundamental measures. That is,

FIGURE 4-1
39-Week MA vs. Dow Industrials*

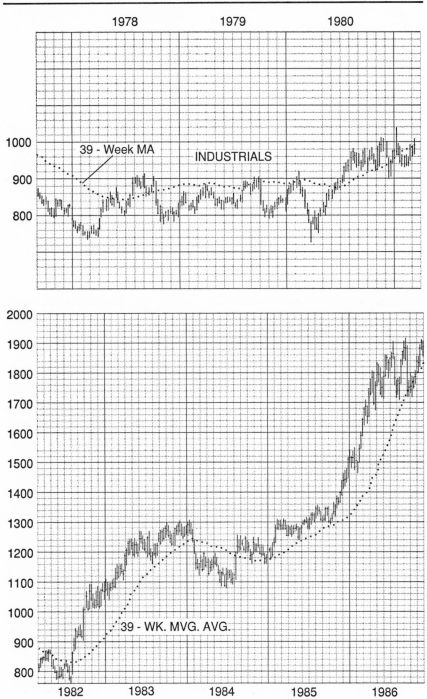

*Source: Securities Research Co., 208 Newbury St., Boston, MA 02116.

they gauge what is going on in the big economic picture, not what is occurring within the markets themselves. We discussed the interaction of the two at some length in our second chapter, and given the importance of these two areas, it's clear they must be factored into any valid market trend model. The description of precisely how we do this is in the respective market chapters coming up.

The final letter, L, in the SIMPL moniker, is a reminder about asset allocation in managing market transactions: Invest in the lowest risk securities for each given market condition. The conditions are decided by proximity to new bull/bear signals and mid-stage confirmations.

In practice, this means that just after a new bull market signal, investments in that market should be made in securities that are relatively low in risk compared to the market itself. This is because market turns are easily the highest risk times to invest and specific holdings should counter this risk until confirmation of a developing bull market comes from other indicators on our list.

At this confirmation juncture, securities with higher risks than the market will be appropriate in order to take advantage of their upside volatility. Market risk itself is lower at this stage than at market turns, so individual issue risk can be increased. (Your own personal risk tolerance will limit this shift to the degree you wish.)

Then, when a first bear market signal is generated, another shift should occur, this back to low-risk issues and increased cash positions, until other indicator confirmations concur. At this downside confirmation, a full cash position is warranted to avoid the bear swipes.

This is the risk control process I noted earlier, and it's a significant element in the whole Right Market Method. It doesn't guarantee excess profits, of course, nor does it rule out any losses. It simply positions your portfolio to minimize risk at the toughest times and maximize rewards at the best.

In performance terms, you can expect it to underperform the market near the bull/bear turns, perhaps for several months, and to outperform it during the confirmed bull periods, assuming they last for multiple months.

This risk control procedure is specified in each market chapter.

The essence of the SIMPL system is, I hope you'll agree, quite simple. Four categories of indicators are used to cross-check one another in identifying the most critical historical ingredients for bull and bear markets. Each category is made up of specific, back-tested indicators that work best for each of our three markets. And, a risk control plan operates throughout the bull/bear cycles. This is the core of the Right Market Method.

We saw earlier how the Fed is the heavyweight player in the U.S. economic game, both by design of Congress and in its own practice. And, that interest rates are the key instruments the Board uses in scoring its points. But we haven't seen exactly *how* these rate switches cause market movements. That's our final building block in selection of specific market indicators and seeing the ultimate point: how startlingly well they've worked.

CHAPTER 5

THE CRITICAL INGREDIENT

Money no longer talks. It goes without saying.—*Anonymous*

Money *really* goes when the Fed intends it to. That's the
ready conclusion those of use who've studied the Fed and its
actions come to. The Fed's pressures on interest rates, especially
upward, have caused more money to disappear then any war
we've fought. Has any war cost us a trillion dollars? That's a
conservative estimate of the amount the Fed wiped out by forcing interest rates higher and helping provoke the bond plunge
and stock Crash of '87.

No, it wasn't only the Fed that caused that crash. Certainly
investor greed relative to stock values, and program trading,
and international financial worries contributed. But neither
would that disaster have happened if interest rates hadn't risen
as dramatically as they did during the spring and summer of
1987. Make no mistake, it was the Fed that caused rates to rise.

As I pointed out in my previous book, *Low Risk Profits in
High Risk Times*, the degree to which the Fed forces interest
rates up or down is an excellent economic/market barometer.
Interest rates, both long- and short-term, measure the pressure
in the financial atmosphere under which the various markets
must operate. It's the Fed that creates the pressures for financial storms and calms.

As most investors know, the general rule about rates and
markets is that the easing of interest rates reduces the pressure on markets, providing a more favorable operating climate,
whereas rising rates put the markets under greater negative
presure. Here's how.

RATES AND PRICES

Hang on for a touch of theory. (If you'd like to skip details, turn to p. 60, "The Chart Evidence".)

Changes in the fixed return on money (which may also be called its *rental* cost to differentiate it from money's *price* in goods and services) should affect investment performance. If the rental rate on any item rises, it will make that item less affordable and will tend to dampen demand for it, and vice versa. In this sense, the rental rate and the actual price perform a similar function. There is no reason to expect that this function should be any different with money than with an automobile or an apartment. In fact, the close adherence of short-term interest rates to inflation rates shown in Figure 5–1 demonstrates the connection between money rental rates (T-bills) and the price of money in goods and services (CPI).

What's more, fixed interest-bearing securities (and the zero coupon variety, as well) actually prove one aspect of this rate-versus-price relationship. When the market rate of return or interest rate rises, those securities with fixed-interest returns must decline in price. Simple mathematics demands it, and the reverse as well.

Another way of seeing the effect of interest rates on investments is by determining what a sum of money (or a bond) that has an exact expected *future* value is worth today.

Assume you are promised that the sum of $100,000 will be paid to you in 20 years and that the payment is certain. There's no risk of nonpayment.

The person or entity that made the promise must now fulfill it. That person is faced with a simple question: How to ensure the money will be there in 20 years? Aside from having it on hand now or hoping for a windfall, there are two solutions. Deposit funds now at a rate of interest that will increase the sum to $100,000 in 20 years. Or deposit an amount periodically at some interest rate to meet the obligation. The amounts and interest rates are mathematically ascertained. Pick a rate of interest, and tables or a calculator will specify the future value of $1 now or $1 periodically paid in through the process of compound interest.

In the first case, if a compound interest rate of 10 percent is selected, $14,864 must be deposited and left to compound *at that rate* for 20 years to equal $100,000. Conversely, the 20-year future sum of $100,000 is "worth" only $14,864 now, assuming the 10 percent interest rate.

Further, if the assumed interest rate were cut in half, to 5 percent, the current value of that 20-year future $100,000 would be well more than double the previous current value: $37,689. The difference in the totals is the effect of compounding at work. The periodic deposit amounts are just as readily calculable as

FIGURE 5-1
3-Month Treasury Bill Rate vs. Consumer Price Index Annual Rate of Change[*]

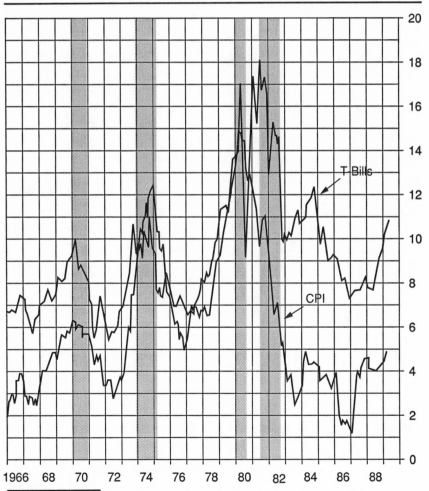

*Source: The Business Picture, op cit., ch. 2.

the fixed amounts.

The important point is that the interest rate, (called the discount rate in such present value calculations), and the time period have precisely determined the present value of some future amount. From this it must be true that not only do interest rates dictate the current value of any future sum, but that somehow this sort of calculation must become part of market expectations for current values of bonds and stocks.

Since notes and bonds have specified periodic payments based on their interest coupons, and since they have fixed maturity dates, a present value for a note's principal and interest payoff must be calculable.

The present value of a $1,000 face-value Treasury note with interest paid at the rate of $100 per year that matures in five years, must be subjected to a discount rate, as above. The discount rate would be the interest rate expected to prevail on *average* in the market for this note over the years to maturity. Let's assume it's 8 percent.

Now, we can do the work on a bond yield calculator, or add the present value of the $100 interest paid in the first year at 8 percent discount to the present value of that interest in the second, third, fourth, and fifth years. To this add the present value at 8 percent of the $1,000 principal payment in the fifth year. This final total will be what the present value of that note should be in the market if rate expectations are 8 percent for that period. If such a note existed and it was selling in the market for *less* than the calculated amount, the market would be expecting rates to average *more* than 8 percent over that period. A higher comparative price would mean market expectations of lower rates.

This is a relatively simple method for determining market comparisons for interest rates on fixed-income securities. The clear result is that changes in interest rates must *directly* affect the *price* of fixed-income securities.

STOCK VALUATIONS

This doesn't work quite as neatly with stocks. As noted earlier, the interest rate-stock price relationship is indirect, but real, nevertheless.

First, interest rates are only one of numerous determinants of stock *values*, including the outlook for earnings and dividends, current prices in terms of historical dividend yields, price to book value, and price/earnings (P/E) ratio, not to mention the market's outlook for the economy, the dollar, and so forth.

Secondly, interest rates and the outlook for them play an important part in key corporate decisions, including the financing of inventories, borrowing for new equipment, and the balance between companies' short- and long-term debt. Thus, the expectations for, and realization of a significant change in interest rates should have a flow-through bearing on corporate profits. Therefore, since stock prices anticipate changes in corporate profits, interest rates must have an indirect bearing on those prices in this way, too.

So, we can say that with stocks there is a flow-through of ideal value to actual price through a perceived trend in short-term interest rates, but first one must determine an ideal value. Here's how that works.

In the formula

$$P = \frac{D}{k - g}$$

D = the dividend amount, P = present value of an infinite stream of dividend income, g = the rate of annual growth of that income, and k = a discount rate for that income in the market. The denominator is kept positive.

Suppose a stock pays a dividend of \$1 per share. If that dividend is expected to be increased 5 percent annually because of the company's projected growth rate, and if it is assumed that this growth should be currently discounted at 8 percent per year on a future-value basis similar to the way note and bond present values have been calculated, then the estimated value for the stock is

$$\frac{1}{.08 - 0.05} = 33.33$$

Naturally, things aren't that simple in the real world. All stocks with this growth rate and dividend don't sell at \$33 per share. In fact, since this formula calculates *value*, it shouldn't be expected to state current price. That still doesn't reduce its worth to us.

The parts of this formula that are least certain are in the denominator factors of k and g: How can one estimate these accurately? Estimating growth for established dividend-paying companies requires a sound consensus of estimates made by analysts and company officers of earnings growth and dividend payout for several years ahead. Although those figures aren't a snap to come by, such estimates are regularly published in brokerage firms' research. They're acceptable for this sort of rough estimation.

Calculating k involves using historical data about the relationship between bond and stock returns. As we saw in Chapter 3, the average stock in the S&P Composite had a total average annual return from 1926 through 1988 of 5.6 percent *above* the long-term government bond return. (The latter, by the way, averaged 1.3 percent above the inflation rate over the period studied.) From this research has been developed a formula using the Capital Asset Pricing Model, which determines the discount rate (k) that brings anticipated equity returns down to present values. It also equals the cost of equity capital to a firm selling stock to investors:

$$k = \text{LBR} + \text{stock to bond return differential} \times \beta$$

where

$LBR =$ long-term government bond rate
$\beta =$ the stock's volatility compared with a market
   volatility of 1.0

Thus the k used in the first formula is figured by adding the current long-term government bond rate, say 0.09, to 0.056 multiplied by 1.0 for a stock that is estimated to be equal in volatility to the overall market. In this case the result is .146.

Inserting this value for k into the previous formula gives

$$\frac{1}{.146 - 0.05} = 10.42$$

That result, compared to the previous one, should provide real food for thought. It's about one-third the previous value.

First, notice that in using a 9 percent government bond rate, k becomes a much larger number than the one derived before. Thus, the equation's denominator became much higher than previously estimated, and the resulting stock price for a $1 dividend was appropriately reduced.

This means that in historical terms a high level of bond interest rates requires that companies grow at faster rates in order to keep their stock prices up. In other words, *stock values will decline with rising bond rates unless company dividend growth rates also increase a similar amount.* (And values will rise under opposite conditions.)

What's more, since bond rates rise when the Fed forces short-term rates higher, it's clear that rising short-term interest rates should eventually lower stock prices. That's exactly what we find true in the marketplace. Once stock *values* fall sufficiently, stock prices follow in due course.

Even more interesting is the point that *anything* which causes the formula's denominator to increase lowers the *value* of stocks. This includes *rising* interest rates, stock to bond return differential and beta. The same result occurs with *falling* dividend growth rates or actual declines in the dividend projection. For our discussion, the change in interest rates is most pertinent in this formula, but I stress again that this deals with stock *value*, not immediately with price.

There's a practical side to this in determining overall stock market values and assumptions within them. On March 31, 1989, the annualized dividends on the Dow Industrial Average totaled $90.64. If we assume that the market was projecting the same k ingredient used in the above formula, for a net denominator of .146, and the Dow stood at 2400, the market was also projecting a 10.8 percent annual dividend growth rate for the Dow. That's roughly the rate dividends in that average had been growing for the two prior years, but was it projectable past 1989 in what was thought to be a slowing economy?

On the other hand, the k ingredient could have been altered by a forecast change in the long-term bond rate to, say, 7 percent. That would put k at .126. If the rise projected in dividend growth was then cut to only 5 percent, the Dow would have a theoretical value of only 1192! Clearly, that was a bad news projection, one the market did not believe in spring 1989.

I caution that not a lot of faith should be put in the *precise* numbers shown by the formula. The accuracy of dividend and bond rate projections doesn't deserve it. But the concept of interest rates driving stock values is valid.

Gold has something of a looser theoretical relationship to interest rates. The connection develops in two ways as we saw in Chapter 2: primarily through changes in inflation rates as perceived by the Fed, to which that body reacts with its interest rate weapon; and by movements in the U.S. dollar abroad, which also may prompt Fed-driven changes in rates.

Accelerations in interest rates tend to be negative for gold because the markets believe the Fed is acting early to stem inflationary pressures. However, during the steep rate rises of 1977–79, the Fed was trailing the inflation increases and rate rises paralleled inflation. Gold then moved up in tandem with inflation all right, but this was contrary to its theoretical pattern versus rising interest rates.

For the 1980s the relationship between short-term rates and gold was shifted by the markets' acceptance of gold as an international alternative to the dollar as a safe haven investment. Therefore, gold has tended to move opposite to the dollar during the past decade.

Of course, there's an interest rate relationship here, too. Rising U.S. rates tend to make the dollar more attractive internationally, pushing it higher against key foreign currencies. A higher dollar price translates to a lower gold price and brings the gold–interest rate connection back to its usual inverse relationship.

In sum, we don't have a neat mathematical relationship between interest rates and the gold market as we do with bonds and stocks. Instead we have more indirect tie.

For this reason, our index of short-term interest rates is not useful in determining gold market trends and we use the inflation and dollar trends as more effective measures.

THE CHART EVIDENCE

Let's look at the 22-year charts of our three markets and the Consumer Price Index changes, Figure 5–2 and an index of short-term interest rates in Figure 5–3 (STIR). It's one I've developed to signal Federal Reserve Board action upon those rates. Its composition is discussed later in the chapter. For now we need note only that it's weighted for the biggest weapon in the Fed's arsenal, the discount rate, at which member banks borrow from the Fed system. On the chart, the index crossovers of its long-term moving average (11 month) provide the trend change signals.

The effect of interest rate trend changes on the markets is easily seen in Figure 5–2. Bond prices nearly always react promptly and inversely to short-term rate changes, sometimes before the crossover signal is generated. Stocks do the same, but usually with a lag after the signal, not at the initial trend change. An exception stands out: 1978–79, which coincided with a sharply rising CPI inflation rate. The market was marking up the value of corporate assets after an initial scare.

Finally, gold also was in the grasp of short-term interest rates in the 1950s and 1960s, but was much less so during the major inflation changes of the 1970s and 1980s.

The chart evidence fits the theory. A clear relationship between short-term interest rate trend changes and each of our markets is observable. And these cycles have no periodicity, that is, no regular pattern.

It's important to understand that I'm not claiming that interest rate cycles will produce X event on Y date in the future. I am saying that short-term interest rate trends can be relied upon to produce an effect on the markets, even if it is not always an immediate one. Therefore, the fact that there are exceptions in stocks and gold does not invalidate the concept. It means that other forces had to have been at work to override the pattern during these periods. We can make allowances for them in judgments about future rate trends, if we can identify the forces.

We should also note that these cycles are sufficient in number to be statistically meaningful (see also Chapter 9). The 1966–88 period shown in Figure 5–2 reveals six-plus complete cycles for stocks and five each for bonds and gold.

With all of this there remains a flaw. The interest rate signals alone are not sufficiently precise in every market to produce optimum transaction results. Good results, yes, especially in the S&P 500. But not in gold mining issues and bonds. Therefore, additional indicators are needed to improve performance, as was

FIGURE 5-2
T-bill, T-bond Yields with CPI Change, S&P 500 Index and Gold Bullion Average Monthly Prices*

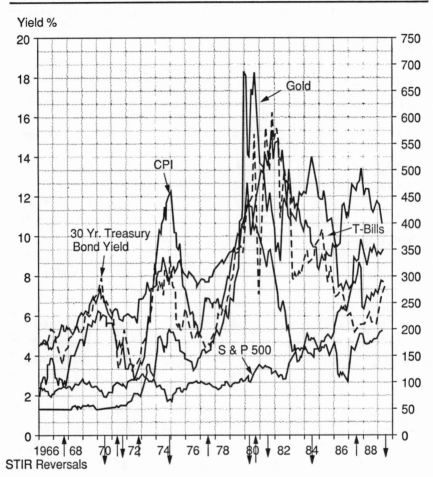

suggested in the previous chapter. This is not the fault of the interest rate cycle. Rather, it's a function of the markets' abilities to *correctly* anticipate rate trends early on. Periodically the markets get it right before a clear trend shows up. This is a potential that we must allow for in making our asset allocation decisions.

*Source: The Business Picture, op cit, Chapter 2.

A STIRing TIME

I've been referring to the Short-Term Interest Rate Index—shortened to STIR Index. It's time to take a closer look at it and how it's used.

The STIR Index, as shown in Figure 5–3, is an index of yields from a small handful of widely quoted money market instruments. As noted, it's weighted toward the biggest tool the Fed has at its disposal, the discount rate—the rate at which member banks borrow from the Federal Reserve System. The Index records what is happening to those money market instruments' yields on a weekly basis.

We then eliminate the meaningless short-term market fluctuations through use of a moving average (MA). The one I've found works best is a 45-week MA. An 11-month MA (shown) is substituted when monthly index values are used. We've also refined this with a 26-week MA, as explained in the next chapter.

Since we understand that all Fed actions either occur directly in, or are quickly reflected by, the money market, STIR trends reveal every week what the Fed is doing in that market. Not only what its members *say* they're doing but what they're actually doing. When STIR crosses its key MA, we know the Fed means the trend to be real.

Occasionally the markets miss the moves, however. Usually they're focused on something else when this occurs, like corporate earnings trends or a recession forecast. On the other hand, and perhaps because of this potential, the Fed has recently been quite clear about its intentions by frequently making public statements on its plans. This has been a hallmark of the Volcker-Greenspan eras, and it contrasts sharply with the policies of their predecessors, who often sought to misdirect the markets as to real Fed intent.

STIR is designed to track the facts, no matter whether the Fed is being devious or not. With STIR there's no speculation. Trends are clear once the Fed puts them meaningfully in place.

A second aspect of this is also important. Figure 5–3 shows just how rarely the Fed changes its mind. Notice how infrequently STIR reverses across its long-term MA: only 14 times in 22 years. Even the shorter blips that run counter to a prevailing trend rarely last longer than a month or two.

The quickest reversal and re-reversal occurred in 1971. A

FIGURE 5-3
STIR Index vs. 11-month MA, 1967–1988*

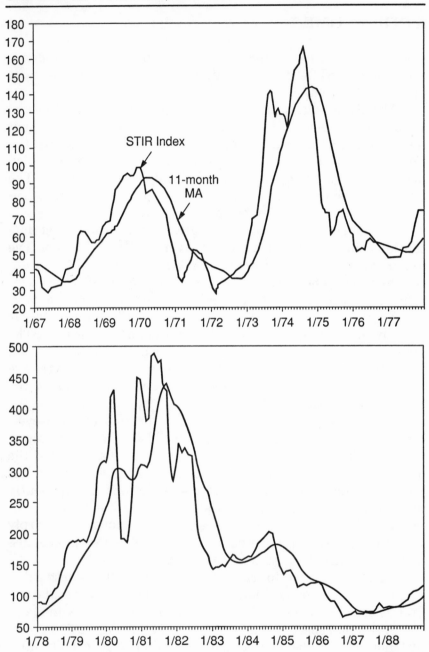

*Source: Kinsman & Associates

falling interest rate trend was reversed to a rising one in April that year, and that rise lasted until November when rates were eased again. Seven months is a long time for most investors. But in the Fed's milieu, seven months is overnight. We discussed the reasons for this in Chapter One.

Recall that this sluggish functioning of the Federal Reserve Board's policies has made investing easier for us. We aren't interested in whether Fed actions are correct, or even whether they're timely enough to solve problems such as rising inflation rates or the speed of computer development. We only want to know what the Fed is doing. It is that which the markets must react to, not what anyone thinks the Fed should be doing. If it takes the Fed six months to figure out whether policy A is correct, fine. STIR tells us when A went into effect, and if it is changed to B.

It may matter in an ultimate sense of our national well-being how well the Fed adapts to the speed of economic change. But in the daily investment world, it doesn't matter. We react to whatever the Fed does in changing or retaining a given policy.

This raises a good question: Don't STIR trackers with an indicator as slow as this tend to miss market moves in stocks, bonds, and gold?

First, investors shouldn't use STIR alone in timing Right Market buys/sells, as we've already stressed. Other indicators can signal actions more quickly than STIR if circumstances demand. But STIR remains the ultimate key.

Second, despite the sensitivity the markets have to interest rates in the 1980s, it's amazing how often some of them ignore STIR trend changes for a time. The stock market is a particularly good example of this. Note in Figure 5–2 how rarely that market made an important turn opposite to the STIR trend change, the direction it should go, before STIR crossed its long-term MA.

The best recent example of the stock market's lag propensity was in signaling the bull market top in 1987. STIR crossed its long-term MA in May, but the market rolled up more than a 15 percent gain after that to its August peak. This leading propensity makes STIR a good forecaster.

The best exception to the rule was 1977 when the market decided to pay attention to the interest rate trend change immediately, some six months before STIR crossed its long-term MA. But note also that there was still nine months left in the market's downside from the MA crossover point before a countertrend rally got underway.

This delay in stock response to STIR trend changes is readily explainable. As noted previously, STIR is an indicator of stock *values*, not necessarily prices. The market can and does ignore value measures from time to time, a fact that value-oriented investors take advantage of. STIR aids in their analysis.

Bonds, on the other hand, are directly affected by STIR trends since their prices are mathematically tied to yield changes. But interestingly, bonds are difficult to trade based on STIR alone. This is because the bond market tends to successfully speculate on Fed policy changes by reading the economic trends correctly, the same thing the Fed is trying to do. Bonds often lead STIR, especially in its MA crossovers, as the chart shows. Again, we use other indicators in conjunction with STIR to determine bond market trends.

Another glance at the gold graph compared to the interest rate trend-measuring STIR shows a distinct lack of correlation in the 1980s, although prior to that the parallel was better, this for the reasons just explained.

A KEY INTEREST RATE VARIABLE:
RATE OF CHANGE

An interesting aspect of the STIR Index is the relationship between the speed of interest rate changes and the trend of the overall economy.

We know that rising interest rates dampen many aspects of economic growth. Consumers willingness to borrow, their ability to afford a home, businesses' capacity to add to inventories or plant and equipment, or even to generate profits are all affected. Now we have evidence that the speed with which rates are forced higher by Fed action affects these abilities, perhaps more than does the size of the increase. That is, it is the *total impact* of the rate change, not just size of a given change alone that appears to have the greatest economic effect.

This can be measured by the steepness of the slope of the rising rate curve over time. In Figure 5–4 are STIR Index upswings from 1954 to 1989, with the percentage gains and the slopes of the increases shown.

The only two rising cycles that did not end in recessions, 1966 and 1984, had the lowest slopes of the nine periods. All others did end in recession.

Note also that the size of the rate change itself—total index gain—does not correlate well with recession results. For example, in the period ending in 1966, a nonrecession year, the total gain was larger than the gains ending in the recession years of 1970, 1974, and 1981. And the second smallest gain, 1981, did involve a recession.

Interestingly, five periods have double digit interest rate slopes. Those ending in 1966, 1970, 1984, and March 1989 do not. As noted, two of the latter did not end in recessions, and they had the lowest slopes of all nine periods (1989 is incomplete). From this, the break at which recessions correlate with rate-rise slopes seems to be something more than the 6 percent for the period ending in 1966, a non-recession sequence, and less than 8 percent, since 1970, a recession year, has a 7.7 percent slope. However, we cannot be certain about this cutoff figure, for the obvious reason that we have only two periods in which the numbers were in the 6–8 percent range, and one resulted in recession, the other not. But the evidence is intriguing.

We must also ask whether there is serious reason to believe that the sharpness of interest rate increases is a valid cause

FIGURE 5–4
Rate of Interest Rate Rises, 1954–1988

Period	Total Index Gain (%)	Slope (%)	Recession?
6/54–10/57	1168	29.2	yes
5/58–12/59	1072	56.0	yes
7/61–11/66	386	6.0	no
6/67–1/70	240	7.7	yes
3/71–8/74	375	12.5	yes
1/77–4/80	782	20.0	yes
8/80–6/81	167	16.7	yes
1/83–8/84	43	2.2	no
9/86–3/89	110	3.7	?

of recessions. The blunt fact is that without other research we cannot be sure. There is a good argument in favor of this, though.

If interest rates rise slowly, they can certainly be absorbed into the planning process by business and probably by individuals to the extent that they plan expenses at all. The moderately rising interest cost becomes just another steadily rising cost of doing business. But sharper increases, just as steep rises in inflation rates, cause at least business to rethink the need for borrowing to spend. Business expenses are under relatively tight scrutiny. We know that deferral of borrowing occurs when profit margins are observably dented by a rise in this expense. Certainly high single or double digit interest rate increases within a year catch financial officers' and CEO's attention. We would expect that sharp rises in a shorter time would do likewise, although the precise point must vary from company to company, and it would be difficult to estimate for the entire economy.

Households probably take this into account in a similar way. If interest rate expenses of the average household are around 20 percent of income, as they have been recently, a 0.5 percent per month (6 percent annual) increase in them is barely noticed. The total household expense rise is only 1.2 percent per year, a mere 0.1 percent per month. Six percent annual inflation would appear to have a similar effect. But double that to 12 percent per year for either inflation or interest expense and it would be far more likely to catch people's attention, especially those considering a major purchase on borrowed money or those with adjustable rate mortgages.

However, there are a host of other factors that come into play in causing an economic slump, ranging from other types of cost increases to falloff in both consumer and business confidence. We simply can't say with certainty that the rate of change in interest rates is *the* critical factor. We can say that the Fed knows rising interest rates cause the economy to slow since that's their method of accomplishing that end.

The best conclusion we can come to is that our data show no decent correlation between total magnitude of rate increases over time and recessions, but an intriguing correlation does exist between the total impact of rate changes and recessions. The exact amount of the rate change needed to cause a recession is more in doubt than is the probability that speed of change itself is part of the cause of recessions.

One final point before we leave the matter of steepness of interest rate rises. Notice the duration of the rate increase cycles in Figure 5–4. They're all lengthy. The average from bottom to peak is two and one-half years of rising rates, with a range of 10 months to a maximum of five years four months. Clearly, the Fed goes after its targets relentlessly, if nothing else.

We're now ready to see where "the rubber meets the road"—how we find budding bull trends in our three markets, using the information we've just discussed and our "every-year" bull market concept.

CHAPTER 6

SCORING IN STOCKS

There are two times in a man's life when he should not speculate—when he cannot afford it—and when he can.— *Mark Twain*

A set of papers landed on my desk recently from the Mutual Fund News Service. That's an outfit that distributes press pitches from mutual funds. Despite the flogging aspect of the information, every now and then something interesting pops up. In this case it was a particular fund's research.

It seems that since September 1969 (the funds' inception), they'd like us to believe that stock selection was an especially tough job. The pitch: Out of 31 of the nation's largest company stocks tracked through year-end 1988, $10,000 invested in the best-performing of the group would have grown to over $514,000. That was Phillip Morris. But, if you'd picked one named International Harvester (now Navistar), it would have left you with only $4,113. Some variance.

Buried in the table used to back up the statements was a surprise. IBM was number 24 of 31 on the list with a total value of just $33,683. That return barely matched inflation over the term. But IBM also happened to be the largest holding of most financial institutions for that 20-year period. So much for genius.

I don't know that these numbers prove anything about the vagaries of individual stock selection. Some investors will do well in picking, some won't. It is a pretty convincing argument that no one can see 20 years ahead, but then who thought they could?

More important in these facts is one argument that the fund was trying to make: An investor should take a long-term view rather than short. And, that it should be done with a diversified list of stocks to avoid the Navistars of the list. How valid is this?

It's safe to say that more has been written about the stock market and ways to beat it than all other markets combined. Any why not? It's the largest market in ownership terms with some 40 million shareholders (even if about half of them own only one share, which we're told is the case).

Strangely enough, seemingly 99 percent of the volumes, treatises, and journals on stocks that I've seen deal with essentially short-term trading methods, not long-term. Perhaps that's more evidence of the "whistling lemon" effect, as promoters and users of stock market systems attempt to satisfy investors' preoccupation with instant action. Trading frequently is also more popular with brokers for the obvious reasons.

Yet, from my personal contact with thousands of investors over the three decades I've been in this business, I can't recall any who've claimed to have made significant profits from *short*-term trading over *long* time frames of, say, a decade or more. A good percentage of those thousands, however, have said they've done quite well with their long-term investments. From this highly unscientific experience, I've gotten the impression that the mutual fund pitch may have something going for it.

A truckload of data backs this up. Take just two small examples: The fact that something in excess of 90 percent of all futures and options traders are net losers has been so widely reported that it's not even argued any longer. And, in the spring of 1989, the U.S. Trading and Investment Championships organization reported that less than *one-quarter* of several hundred entrants each year in its annual contests show *any profits* at all. The contests pick the best *short-term* performers in categories including stocks, options, and futures.

Those aren't proofs, of course, but they are compelling ideas.

In fact, there's no way of proving why this discrepancy between long-term and short-term results exists. After all, there are big long-term losers, too, as the Navistar anecdote suggests. My educated guess is that since short-term trading methods must inherently be based on short-term market conditions, they'll be geared to those factors creating a specific bull or bear trend, or a segment of it, not to multiple cycles of both. Naturally, these factors change often in our dynamic economy, and when they do, trading methods based on them become obsolete or, at a minimum, obsolescent. Goodbye, short-term profits.

Whatever the true reason behind the apparent popularity and rapid decline of fast buck profits, it's clear that many longer-term market approaches have endured. The concepts and methodology behind ideas such as those of Graham and Dodd in *Securities Analysis*, Gerald Loeb in *The Battle For Investment Survival*, and Charles Allmon in his advisory letter, *The Growth Stock Outlook*, to name a few, have all been around for decades and are still going strong.

Interestingly, these are all "value" approaches to the stock market. They look at such mundane subjects as balance sheets, dividend coverage by earnings, and a host of accounting and market financial ratios. In doing so, they implicitly recognize that value in stocks *takes time* to be realized.

This isn't to say that technical approaches to the markets, many of which are short-term, are conceptually weak. Quite the contrary, some of them appear to be highly substantive. The grandfather tome of this method, the 40-year-old *Technical Analysis of Stock Trends* by John Magee, has stood the test of time and gains new readers every year. It has spawned a plethora of imitators and revisionists but it remains the true technicians' bible. The truth is that technical analysis, in its serious form, when handled by real students of the subject, has come of age in the 1980s.

In fact, the primary differences between the two approaches are that the technical method is newer than fundamental analysis, and its tools, charts, numbers, and angles can be used to develop *either* short-term or longer-term buy/sell decisions. The value approach inherently focuses on the longer range because it is only with time that value will "out."

Whatever your orientation, short-term or long, it's really not a function of how much more money might be made with one or the other. It's truly a function of temperament. Some people just like life in the fast lane, no matter where it takes them. They'd never be happy with a long-term investment approach, except as a back-to-the-wall recourse after losing a bundle. Others just can't think in terms of fast action. Quick decisions and high turnover are an anathema to them. They're long-term investors whether they like it or not. And these considerations are the ones you should address in deciding your approach.

Our Right Market Method for stocks takes something from both the fundamental value and technical schools, and thereby has a few shorter-term aspects mixed with the predominant long-term. It uses the economic fundamentals of interest rates and consumer prices, similar to those used by value finders, and adds such technical staples as moving averages, sentiment statistics, and forecasting formulas. Perhaps this tapping of both worlds is one reason for RMM's success.

The most important fact to remember about RMM is that it has a definite long-term market bias. It doesn't rely on trading to generate its profits, as I've stressed earlier. In stocks, it signaled only *eight* buy/sell combinations in the 22 years through early 1989 that we've used as our explanatory period. And, with all three key market trades counted, it's only produced 18 combinations in the same period—less than one buy-sell per year on average. I believe that qualifies as long-term. Moreover, it emphasizes a "sleep well" attitude for investors, through its inherent risk control methodology. That too is a characteristic of a long-term, not short-term, orientation.

In addressing stocks, RMM focuses on broad moves of the overall market, which as we've seen, have been shown to statistically account for about 60 percent of the price movement of the average stock. This readily allows for the use of stock mutual funds as the profit-generating vehicles during signaled bull markets. And the stage of development of the bull market (early, confirmed, or late) tells us the degree of volatility inherent in the type of fund we'll buy, or in the type of stock to buy.

Indeed, this approach does support the purchase of individual stocks after bull market signals, but RMM itself does not make the selections. An RMM adjunct that we have developed for my *Low–Risk GROWTH Letter* acts as a stock screen for that purpose. Instead, RMM tells us when there is a high degree of probability that any stock selection process has the most going for it—a bull market—and when it will be least rewarding or outright dangerous—a bear market. Thus, it is fully compatible with (1) mutual fund investing, (2) its own adjunct buying screen, or (3) any other sound stock selection process. This makes *flexibility* one of the RMM hallmarks.

Actually, our approach has a further inherent selection advantage. Because two of our stock bull market indicators forecast the trends in interest rates and inflation, investors automatically know when conditions are favorable or unfavorable for interest-sensitive stocks like utilities, preferreds or banks, and inflation-sensitive issues like precious metals, natural resources, or oils. When a bull market signal is flashed for stocks or gold, investments in the respective individual issues or in sector mutual funds that represent the interest-sensitive or resource stocks, respectively, then becomes an automatic alternative to buying general funds or other specific value stocks.

Further, that "value method" of individual stock selection works especially well with our RMM, although it does so best during the early and confirmed stages of stock bull runs. That long-term nature of both processes appears to be exactly the reason for this. Each allows time for value to be recognized by the market. The key difference is that RMM will tell investors when to be entirely out of stocks. Some value approaches remain heavily invested under all conditions.

In sum, once our approach has identified the big picture bull trends for the overall stock market and certain sectors within it, the largest part of the job is done. The refinement can be undertaken individually thereafter by any method of your choice, or with The Low-Risk GROWTH Letter stock screen.

THE INDICATORS

Now let's get down to the critical question: Which signals catch the stock bull-bear market moves best? And how?

We've already discussed the theory behind each type of indicator we use in our SIMPL system. However, the consumer price inflation category deserves further comment in regard to stocks.

This factor is important to stocks in three ways: one is through its affect on bond prices, which is clearly negative as inflation accelerates because it must affect the stock value formula, $V = d/(k - g)$, noted in the previous chapter. Closely allied, an inflationary acceleration usually prompts Fed action to raise interest rates, reinforcing the bond negative.

A third way inflation hits is through corporate earnings. But this is a mixed pressure. An acceleration in inflation, depending somewhat on from which source it develops, initially impacts negatively on most corporate earnings because companies tend to be more reactive to cost increases in raising prices than to be initiators of price increases on their own. For a period just following an inflation acceleration, then, corporate earnings are negatively impacted as costs rise. This may reverse soon, as companies raise prices in offsetting moves. This also extends the spread of inflation as the offset increase affects the responding firms' customers.

Once the price rise process is underway, however, it tends to benefit some, particularly those companies that have extensive inventories, in that it makes the goods on the shelf more profitable when they're sold.

Proof of this market reaction to inflation comes from Figure 6–1 showing, in the postwar era, the decline in the multiple that the market places on stocks' earnings per share as inflation rises. Clearly, low levels of inflation are associated with high multiples, up to the 22 times area. But bring inflation rates

FIGURE 6–1
Inflation Rates vs. Stock P/E Multiples, 1949-1985

Inflation Range %	Average P/E	P/E Range
0.0 to 2.0	15.8	21.7–9.8
2.1 to 4.0	14.1	18.5–8.8
4.1 to 6.0	12.1	17.6–7.2
6.1 to 8.0	12.2	16.4–9.3
8.1 to 10.0	10.4	14.2–8.4
Above 10.0	8.2	8.9–7.5

Source: Gerald Perritt, *Small Stocks, Big Profits* (Dow Jones-Irwin, 1988) p. 3.

up to recent levels of 4 percent to 6 percent, and that multiple drops to an *average* of 12.1.

Statistically, the market's PE multiple drops by about 0.7 for every one percentage point increase in the inflation rate. This is historically speaking, not the instant reaction of the market to a belief in higher inflation rates.

The net is that inflation accelerations are a mixed blessing in the business world, but their initial affect is negative on most corporate profits. Obviously, this creates an early negative tendency for stocks. Accordingly, early knowledge of inflation rate changes are important to the onset and demise of stock bull and bear markets, and the use of an indicator to catch them is fully appropriate for our method.

However, given the mixed nature of the inflationary pressure and its historical affect on stocks, we also can assume it is not as strong a negative as a rising interest rate trend. That's got pure math going for it.

Now, how do we measure inflationary changes in a way that the stock market responds to?

The most obvious way, a straight reading of changes in the Consumer Price Index (CPI), isn't sufficient. Figure 6–2 shows the S&P 500 Stock Index from 1966 onward, with the year-over-year change in consumer prices superimposed. This form of CPI change did a fine job in alerting investors to market turns, on the basis that a rise in the CPI change meant a market decline was upcoming, and vice versa, *until 1978*. At that point of the greatest inflation takeoff in modern history, the stock market followed suit until late 1980. Then, with the inflation rate falling, so did the market. Two contrary cycle failures is enough to invalidate an indicator for me. But it added insult in 1987, when the CPI rate soared and so did the market, at least until that infamous month. This format for inflation measurement was a nice idea but gave us no cigar.

There are many other measures of inflation, from those contained in the government's quarterly GNP report (implicit deflator and fixed weight deflator), to producer prices and a forecasting indicator we'll address with the gold market, the Leading Index of Inflation. We've researched each of these and found no joy. They just don't forecast stock trends.

Suspecting that the problem was one of measurement

FIGURE 6–2
Consumer Price Index (Annual change) vs. S&P 500 Stock Index*

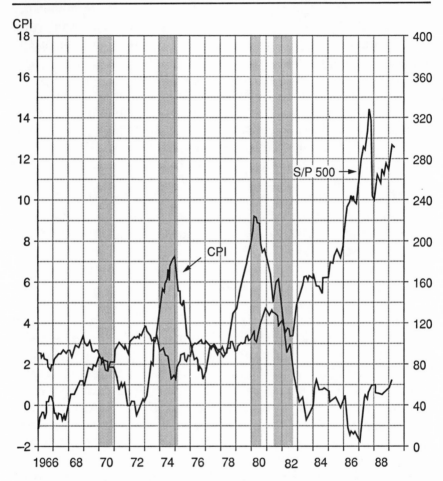

method rather than the validity of the idea itself, with the aid of our computer we came across a way of tracking the CPI itself that does indeed give a reasonable indication of future stock trends. It's not flawless as to timing, but then we don't expect any one indicator to be. That's why we use more. But it has been correct on each major stock trend since 1972, it's initial tracking year. We've named it the Weighted CPI (W.CPI) to

*Source: The Business Picture, op. cit, ch. 2.

FIGURE 6–3
The Stock Sensitive Inflation Measure, W.CPI, with Signals 1972–1989

Date	Action	S&P Level
October 1972	rising : sell	109.6
February 1975	falling : buy	80.1
March 1977	rising : sell	100.6
August 1980	falling : buy	123.5
September 1983	rising : sell	167.2
December 1984	falling : buy	164.5
October 1986	rising : sell	237.4
January 1988	falling : buy	250.6
August 1988	rising : sell	263.7
January 1989	falling : buy	285.4
April 1989	rising : sell	302.6

reflect a weighting of the numbers within the indicator to give more significance to those ocurring recently than to those of several months ago.

W.CPI's calls versus each month's average value of the S&P 500 shows its success. The data in Figure 6–3 are for the month in which the CPI was publicly reported.

Not a loss among the group, although in fairness, most of the period showed rising stock prices. Nevertheless, a check of the record against the stock chart in Figure 6–2 shows that the only temporary mistakes were too early a favorable sign in August 1980 and too soon an unfavorable signal in October 1986.

When compared to the CPI percent change on the same chart, the record is even more favorable. W.CPI called all of the important changes in inflation trend without exception.

In fact, the strongest critique of this indicator is that it has appeared lately to be almost too sensitive to inflation changes, generating four signals in the 15 months to April 1989. However, as the chart shows, inflation itself also flip-flopped, so W.CPI is doing exactly the job it was designed for.

You can calculate the W.CPI for yourself with the help of a computer. (See the Appendix.)

The W.CPI is figured by taking the percentage change of

the CPI itself from the *current* month compared to its prior 12 months' average level. By doing this for each month of a year we get a first 12-month moving average of the percent changes, which is multiplied by a constant (2) to ready it for comparison to a second MA. (You can check on how to calculate a MA in Chapter 4 if needed.) Then, the most recent four months of this MA are weighted double original value in figuring a second moving average of the percent changes. The second MA is then compared to the first MA. When the *difference* between the two *exceeds* a 5 percent filter, a signal is generated: a rising-sell signal when the excess is higher, a falling-buy when it's lower.

Figure 6–4 shows readings and signals for the W.CPI calculations during spring 1988. In March, the MA percent charge was more than 5 percent below the weighted MA, giving a favorable signal, +1. In April, the comparison was less than 5 percent either way (equal), for a reading of zero, neutral. By July, the MA percent change had reversed to a level more than 5 percent above the weighted MA, calling for rising inflation— a negative signal. That later reversed to a buy with W.CPI's December reading, right in time for the major rally of 1989. Note, however, that the months referred to in the table are those for which the CPI was reported, not the month the report was issued—one month later.

The Other Two Key Indicators

Remember, we do not use just a single indicator to tell us a market trend change, even though the one we've just seen would have done quite well on its own. Never showing a loss

FIGURE 6–4
Examples of W.CPI Readings

Date (1988)	CPI	12MMA	MA%C	Wtd.MA	Signal
March	116.5	114.7	3.7	4.1	+1
April	117.1	115.1	4.1	4.1	0
May	117.5	115.4	4.2	4.1	0
June	118.0	115.8	4.4	4.2	0
July	118.5	116.2	4.6	4.3	−1

through more than five complete bull/bear cycles is a pretty high accomplishment. But, no single trend forecaster will work under *all* conditions.

The second stock indicator is one we've already discussed, our proprietary measure of short-term interest rates, the STIR Index. Its construction is also shown in the Appendix.

Recall that as a measure of the interest rate pressure the Fed controls over the markets, STIR movements must affect the bond component of the stock value formula shown in the theory discussion in Chapter 5. That means its readings are inverse to the expected stock trend: a rising STIR equates with falling stocks and vice versa. However, remember also that in the formula it is stock *values* with which we're dealing, so the market must recognize an aggregate change in value before changing price. I happen to believe that interest rates are the most important of the value measures, but the market doesn't always (most of the time?) care what I believe!

In any case, this means that STIR trend changes tend to allow thoughtful action. They don't generate midnight telegrams demanding action.

Since STIR is an index that develops long-range trends, recall that two moving averages work well in signaling true changes: a 26-week (6-month) alert and a 45-week (11-month) final signal. The latter is shown in Figure 6–5.

STIR itself is calculated weekly from data provided by the Federal Reserve, and I've found that when STIR is about to move through its long-term moving average in a direction that would create a signal that's *contrary* to the market's current trend, it's useful to wait until at least that month's end to insure the STIR trend is valid. The market won't believe it anyway, so the delay usually works in our favor.

Note the exception to this in 1977 when the market averages topped in January and the official rising rate signal didn't come until the end of May. May was still a fine time to sell since the market low didn't occur for another nine-and-a-half months. But STIR started its uptrend in January and crossed its *alert* MA in March, giving a clear warning that a pattern change was likely. Meanwhile, the Dow and S&P 500 were generally declining during these months, but the fall was modest.

So we treat an interest rate trend change that is *paralleling* what the market *should* be doing with that change, as generat-

FIGURE 6–5
STIR Signals vs. S&P 500

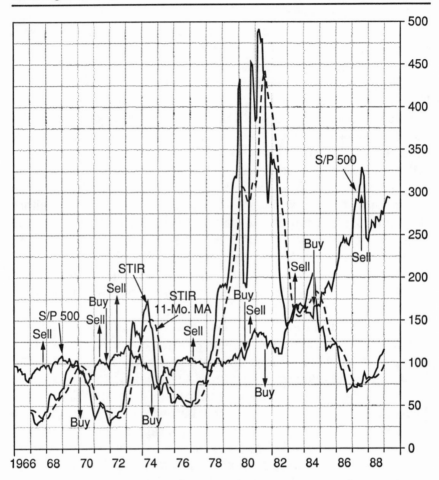

ing a *half-point* plus or minus reading *at the crossover of the 26-week MA,* without waiting for the final cross of the long-term MA at a month's end. (See Stock Model discussion in the next section.)

Since STIR uses and ramifications were discussed at length in prior chapters, we can move on to the two of our four basic indicator types remaining in the SIMPL system: market momentum and sentiment. Momentum is the third of our key ingredients and it's both easy to figure and to track.

The widely accepted 200-day moving average of a stock market index like the Dow Industrials or the S&P 500 gives us a fair measure, although some prefer working with a 39-week version. The former is shown in *Investor's Daily* each weekday, and we carry it in our service and hotline. As a measure of the longer-term market trend it's most useful. The reason that it aids our discovery of bull/bear trends is that it recognizes the market itself is a pretty good forecaster of what's going on in the economy and with corporate profits. It obviously overreacts to some straws in the wind, but, on the whole, it is a very worthwhile indicator of trends. Accordingly, knowing what it's saying can be a valuable ingredient in deciding upcoming bull/ bear turns.

We've found, however, that a small filter on the 200-day MA is required because at important turns, when the market average tends to muddle around the MA for a time, direct movements across the line can whipsaw back and forth. Our filter is 2 percent: When the market average crosses the 200-day MA by that amount, it's a valid turn. You can recheck the 39-week version of this MA in action in Figure 4–1.

COMBINING THE THREE KEYS

The three key stock indicators can now be combined in the simplest possible way: When any *two* of them call a market trend in the same direction, an action signal is given. Falling inflation and interest rates and a market rise above its 200-day MA are bullish for stocks. Rising inflation and interest rates and a market fall below its 200-day MA are bearish. These three form the Stock Market Model in our Right Market Method, and any two of them in bullish or bearish camps say "act." (Model reading +2). (Note that the half-point signal from a STIR break through its 26-week MA is a special case. Use it to take small stock positions on declining breaks and to reduce positions on rising crossovers.)

The sentiment measure is the Bullish Consensus (BC) for stock index traders. Because of its short-term orientation, it's used to fine tune buy/sell transactions, not as a key indicator itself. It stands outside the action model and is triggered into use only when the model has spoken. Here's how.

BC indicates when stock index traders are becoming excessively bullish, or bearish, or just neutral. Naturally, they're in the latter mood most of the time. The record of when they are heavily bullish or strongly bearish is very sharp: The traders are wrong. This has nothing to do with their being ignorant or misinformed. It's largely a function of the systems they use to become bullish or bearish, because they tend to be trend-following in nature. That means more traders will become bullish when a rising trend is underway than at the time just before or exactly at the moment it started. And when the trend is truly strongest and "everyone" has joined in, the bullish optimism is the greatest. That's also when all, or nearly all, money is already committed. Everyone has bought. And that's a great definition of a market top. BC picks these better than any indicator. When the exact reverse occurs, it's a bottom, and BC's splendid on these, too.

Two examples from that wonderful testing year, 1987: The BC reached its highest level of the year, 69 percent bullish, the exact week of the market's peak, August 25, after having registered its second highest reading only two weeks before, at 66 percent. BC also hit its lowest mark of '87 the day after Black Monday, just 27 percent.

Figure 6-6 shows the weekly BC percent of stock index traders bullish for 1988, compared with the Dow Industrials. In this trading range year, bounded by about Dow 1900 and 2200, note the largest Dow moves were exactly *paralleled* by the BC trend: February up, March down, May–June up, August down, especially October–November down to the low for the year, and the final December rally.

The trick with the BC is setting marks for what is excessively bullish or bearish. In 1987 there were several weeks of readings of 60 percent and greater and several in the mid-30 percent range, including four weeks immediately after the August peak. It turns out that two factors provide good interpretations of the BC: its actual trend and its *second* 12-month high/low. A rising or falling *BC trend* of 2–3 weeks is a good indication of a market that will follow suit. And readings in the

FIGURE 6-6

Bullish Consensus vs. Dow Industrials, 1988

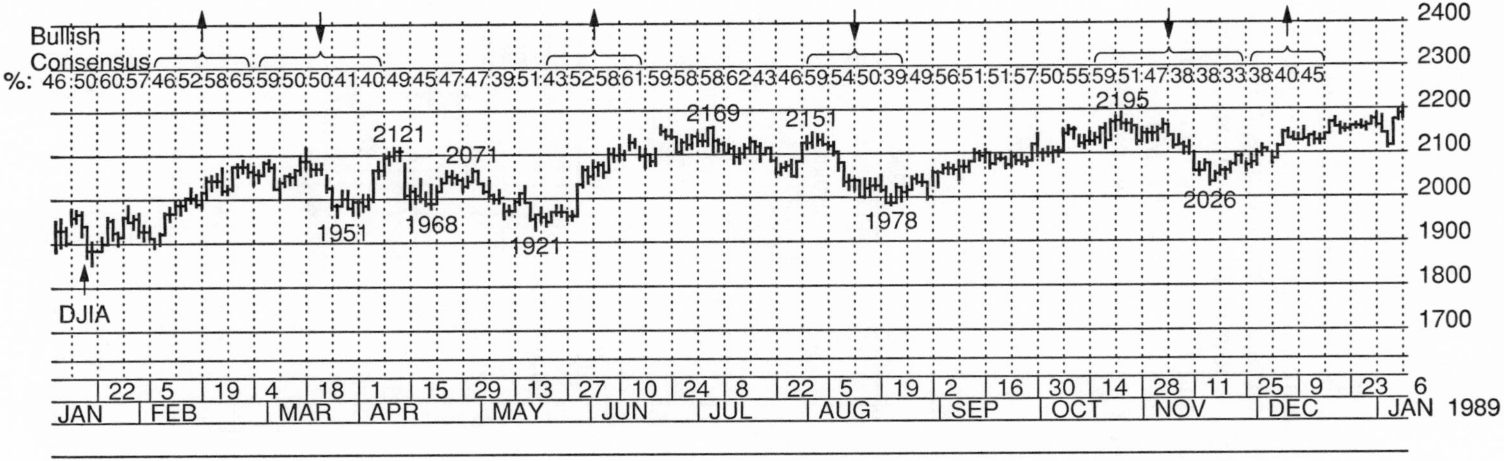

BC figures that reach 12-month highs or lows, followed by a *second* high-low reading outside recent levels, are strong indications of interim or major tops/bottoms. Sales should be made on the *second* high or low in the sequence.

As we're not using BC as a key indicator in the Model, but rather to time transactions after the Model has generated its buy or sell, we don't need to fine tune further than these rather

FIGURE 6–7
Stock Market Model Signals, 1982–1985

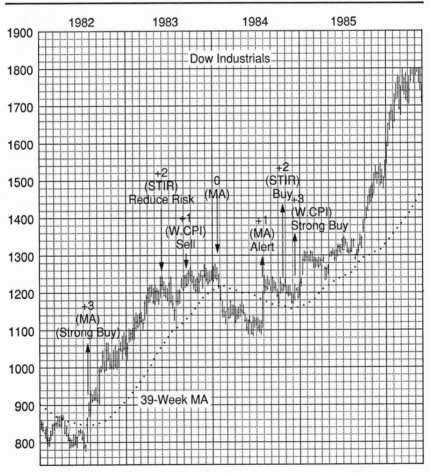

rough guidelines. We know the Model's buy or sell signal is likely to be near a very satisfactory level already. BC is the icing.

THE INDICATOR RECORD

Let's act on our indicators. We now take note of the stock market's three development stages: early, confirmed, and late. They correspond to the Stock Model's number of indicator signals *after the first one*. That is, if only one of the basic three—STIR, W.CPI or 200-day MA—turns positive, there is no buy signal, only an alert. But when a second one moves to plus, that is a buy signal for the *early* stage of a bull market. Then, the third positive indicator gives us a *confirmed* bull to charge with. This is the segment of the market move that usually produces the greatest gains.

The *late* market stage is signaled when, after all three are positive, one of them turns negative. That's the first sell signal. A second negative indicator creates a full sell, to bring stock holdings to zero. We'll specify exact rules for the signals in a moment.

Figure 6–7 shows the 1982–1985 period on the Dow chart, while Figure 6–8 shows the complete signal set for stocks since 1967, including percentage gains.

Let's microscope the 1982–85 period.

All three indicators were positive through May 1983, giving us a *confirmed* bull market reading. It had been in existence since August 1982, when the Dow crossed its 200-day MA at the 860 level. The Model was previously in its early stage position (+2) from October 1981 when STIR kicked positive, joining an already positive W.CPI. The Dow stood at 820 for the initial buys in 1981.

In June 1983, STIR flipped negative, bringing the Model to a +2 reading and beginning the sell process. (See Rules below.) The Dow was at the 1240 level late in June when the indicator turned, bringing our gain to 44 percent following the confirmed bull signal and 51 percent from the earlier +2 stage.

In September, W.CPI turned negative with the Dow near

the 1260 level. That brought the Model reading to +1 and an outright sell. Finally, in January 1984, the Dow's 200-day MA was crossed at Dow 1220, and the Model stood at zero. The final low was around Dow 1080.

In 1984 the process began to reverse when the W.CPI turned neutral in June (not shown). In August, with the sharp market rise, the MA was taken out for a +1 Model reading. It was joined in October by STIR's plus, taking us to a +2 total and an early stage buy with the Dow back around 1220.

The confirmation of a major bull market came in December with the W.CPI plus and Model at +3, with the Dow at 1200. We should now become fully invested, and in fact began to make those last commitments in our December 1984 *Low-Risk GROWTH Letter.*

This positioned us nicely for the 1985–87 massive bull run of 1,500 Dow points. Not until October 1986 did any indicator turn negative, and it was W.CPI that did it first with the Dow at 1880. That generated a first sell signal—obviously early. By late May 1987, STIR had turned negative, giving us a second sell signal from a Model +1 reading, with the Dow at 2300. We advised stock sales into market strength at that time, reaching a 70 percent cash position by September 1 and the Dow near its peak over 2700.

The further deterioration of the STIR in September and the downward thrust of the Dow towards its 200-day MA, allowed us to call for a *major bear market* on our October 15, 1987 hotline. The Dow closed at *2480* that day. This was after we forecast "a substantial decline" if the Fed didn't reverse the upward interest rate push, during a Financial News Network interview on October 6. October 16 saw the Dow break its 200-day MA, giving us a zero Market Model reading.

SENTIMENT

The Bullish Consensus could have been factored into these trades, although we weren't using it in our recommendations at the time. You'll recall that we're looking for a BC two- to three-week trend or a second yearly high or low.

FIGURE 6–8
Complete Stock Market Signals, Jan. 1967–Apr. 1989

Date Date		Signal	Action	S & P Average	Gain	Time
Jan. '67		STIR down				
Jan. '67		MA (up)	Buy	85.04		
Nov. '67		STIR up				
Jan. '68		MA (down)	Sell	95.04	11.8%	12 mo.
Mar. '70		STIR down				
Sep. '70		MA (up)	Buy	82.58		
Jul. '71		STIR up				
Jul. '71		MA (down)	Sell	99.0	19.8%	10 mo.
Nov. '71		STIR down				
Dec. '71		MA (up)	Buy	99.17		
Aug. '72		STIR (up)				
Oct. '72		W.CPI up				
Feb. '73		MA (down)	Sell	109.6	10.5%	10 mo.
Oct. '74		STIR down				
Jan. '75		MA (up)				
Feb. '75		W.CPI down	Buy	72.56		
Jan. '77		MA (down)				
Mar. '77		W.CPI up				
May '77		STIR up	Sell	100.6	38.6%	24 mo.
May '80		STIR down				
May '80		MA (up)	Buy	107.7		
Aug. '80		W.CPI down				
Nov. '80		STIR up				
Jun. '81		MA (down)	Sell	132.3	22.8%	13 mo.
Oct. '81		STIR down				
Aug. '82		MA (up)	Buy	109.7		
Jun. '83		STIR up				
Sep. '83		W.CPI up	Sell	167.2	52.4%	13 mo.
Jan. '84		MA (down)				
Aug. '84		MA (up)				
Oct. '84		STIR down	Buy	164.8		
Dec. '84		W.CPI down				
Oct. '86		W.CPI up				
May '87		STIR up	Sell	286.8	74.0%	31 mo.
Oct. '87		MA (down)				
Jun. '88		MA (up)				
Jan. '89		W.CPI down	Buy	285.4		
Apr. '89		W.CPI up	Sell	302.6	6.0%	3 mo.
Compound gain:					608.5%	114 mo.
Buy–Hold gain:					255.8%	262 mo.

June 1983 initial sale, BC weekly percentage readings: 60, 66, 88, 79. Sale made on second high during fourth week because prior 12-month high was 85 percent (not shown).

September '83 second sale, percentages: 40, 64, 77, 59. Sale made into continuing strength in third week.

October '84 initial buy, percentages: 61, 28, 52, 58, 69. Buy made in third week, after the decline reversed.

December '84 second buy, percentages: 43, 30, 26, 57. Buy made in third week's decline.

October '86 initial sale, percentages: 32, 36, 46, 40, 48. Sale made after strength in third week.

May '87 second sale, percentages: 52, 43, 48, 51. Sale made into fourth week's strength.

As you see, the BC regularly provides at least a two-week trend in the direction we wish, although it may require a couple of weeks' wait. The 12-month high/low rule came into play only once, that during the June 1983 sale. It caught the market's interim peak to the week. When the high-low rule is triggered, it demands action immediately.

LESSONS FROM THE STOCK SIGNALS

The signals form eight pairs of buy/sell combinations covering more than 6 cycles since 1967, which is statistically sound. This approach beat a buy-hold strategy despite RMM's receiving no credit for earnings while *out* of stocks, which RMM was 57 percent of the time.

This leads to an important observation: The Right Market approach requires *patience* to work well. The average time invested per buy/sell combination is 14.3 months, with a range of 3 to 31 months. And the average time out of stocks is greater: 21 months. Still, the method did catch the correct side of all the major bull and bear markets in the period without error, as shown in Figure 6–9. What's more, the RMM investments while out of stocks showed superior results. Our *total* gains from all three markets over the 22 years was *ten times* the stock buy-hold gain.

FIGURE 6–9
Stock Market Model Signals on S&P's 500 Stock Index*

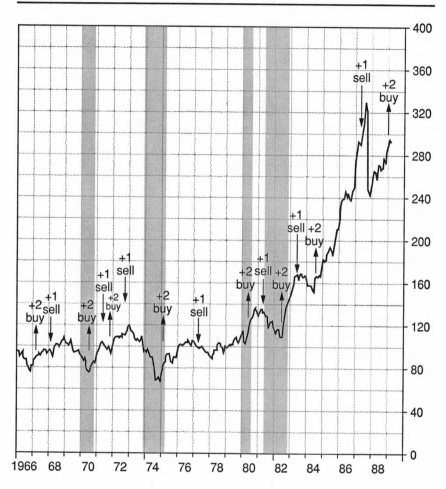

*Source: Courtesy of The Business Picture, op. cit. Ch. 2.

The lead times to market trend changes offered by RMM further emphasize the need for patience in its use. With most RMM buy-sell signals there will be a time when the signal *appears wrong*—it's going against the trend. This means that discipline is necessary: One must believe in the correctness of the signal and determine to wait the market out.

This also offers a distinct advantage. Investors need not jump headlong into or out of the market at a buy or sell signal, but can generally increase or decrease positions following the signals. This is also a risk control factor and is precisely what we do in our exact plan for following RMM in stocks.

Patience, when you have good alternatives, pays off.

THE EXACT PROFIT PLAN

Investors primarily seeking capital growth should follow this Right Market Method plan, based on our Stock Market Model. (Those requiring maximum income see the next section, "For Income Investors Only.")

1. When the Model flashes one favorable signal, an *alert* to buy is advised, but no action is required then.

2. A second favorable Model signal says "buy" now. This is the *early stage* initial buy and requires that the purchase be made in issues that are *lower in risk* than the overall market.

These include those with statistical risk (betas) of around 0.7 to 0.9 versus the market level of 1.0. These numbers are available from brokers and in the *Value Line* and *Daily Graphs* services. A description of risk measurement is in the Appendix.

• The purpose of this is simply risk control at a time in the market cycle when its risk is relatively high, so yours should be lowered.

• A widely diversifed stock fund meeting these risk criteria is appropriate, as are utility and other interest sensitive stocks IF one of the two favorable Model signals is STIR.

• Examples of large, no-load mutual stock funds that fit the risk criteria are Vanguard's Windsor, Windsor II, and Wellington; T. Rowe Price's Growth & Income; Fidelity Equity Income; and Value Line Income.

• The amount of your assets used for this purchase should be in line with the Asset Allocation rules in Chapter 10, depending on whether other markets are in bull stages.

3. Maximum market exposure and the highest relative level of risk should be taken when the Model signals a third positive reading. This is the *confirmed* bull market stage, and the market risk is lower than at the early stage. You can afford to take greater risk in your holdings. If you're an investor who can accept above market risk, statistical levels of 1.25 betas and up are appropriate. It not, stay in the 1.0 area. The amount invested will be dictated by our Asset Allocation rules.

Large family no-load stock funds that are in the higher risk range include Vanguard's Explorer and Naess & Thomas Special, T. Rowe Price's New Horizon, Fidelity's Growth Fund and Freedom Fund, and Value Line Leveraged Growth. Also, 20th Century's Select and Ultra fit this risk range.

The funds of those groups with average market risk include Vanguard's Index Trust and Trustees' Commingled Equity, T. Rowe Price's Growth Stock, Fidelity Fund and Magellan, and Value Line Fund.

Note that these are examples only. Specific recommendations at the time of Model signals are included in my *Low-Risk GROWTH Letter* and advisory service. They do follow these guidelines, but may include other funds, such as closed-end issues, and individual stocks. See also the Appendix for Approved Stock Funds.

4. When negative signals begin to unfold, the rule is to cut back risk first. If the Model switches to a +2 from a +3 by one indicator turning negative, such as in October 1986, this is a *late stage* bull market and you should switch from higher-risk/aggressive holdings to the lower risk category noted above. This makes the +2 Model reading the same no matter if it's on the way up or down. +2 says lower risk issues, period.

5. When the Model *drops* to a +1 reading, your action is different than if it *rises* from zero to +1. In the decline mode you should begin the process of selling your holdings into market strength, just as we did in my service in summer 1987. There is no hard rule on how to do this, but a rule of thumb should be that following our Model's declining signal to a +1, any day the Dow or S&P 500 reaches a new high that's 5 percent above its previous high, sell 1/3 of your holdings.

• The final all-out-of-the-water signal is when the Model reaches a zero reading, at which time all stock positions should be sold immediately.

When you follow these five rules with stocks, you'll have achieved better-than-professional investor status! You'll be one up because this discipline is tighter than most pros can follow. You don't have to have a committee meeting to act, and the positions you're acting on probably won't disturb the market. Average investors do have real advantages, after all.

More importantly, you won't be following the crowd in using the Right Market Method. You'll be following a two-decade proven winner that the crowd will probably ignore.

FOR INCOME INVESTORS ONLY

The above plan for growth-oriented investors is easily modified for those who require investment income on which to live. The simple way is to buy stocks with high dividend yields at the time of the Stock Model's +2 reading, the early bull market. But this leaves you on your own in the stock selection process.

A better approach is to use those diversified stock funds listed above in paragraph 2 which are combined growth and income or straight income funds. They will offer yields that are above average for that market stage. So will straight utility stocks and funds specializing in them.

This still has the disadvantage of not likely being able to maximize income production compared to that available from the bond market. Since stock and bond bull markets have a strong tendency to move together, the best alternative for those needing the highest SAFE income possible, is to use the Bond Model Income Plan shown in the next chapter.

However, those of you who wish to hold stocks and are adequately supported by the income from them, perhaps on the probability that capital growth will permit greater income production in the future should expect to invest about 2/3 of your liquid assets in those issues at the time of the +2 Model reading. The balance should be invested in a combination of one- to three-year maturity Treasury notes for the time being.

When the Model signals a +3 reading, the confirmed bull market, the Treasury notes can be sold with proceeds converted to income stocks or stock funds, or held to continue income production. Your choice.

As the stock market reaches its late stage with a reversion to the +2 reading, a cutback to 50 percent in income stocks/funds and 50 percent money market fund should be made. Now is the time to begin capturing some of your capital gains and protecting them for future income production. This stage and/or the +1 stage may last for an extended period. During these stages the probability of rising interest rates is high, as was the case from late 1986 to early October 1987 and from summer 1988 to spring 1989. So holdings in money funds are apt to show increasing income.

The zero Model reading is a definite "head for the exits" signal for income investors, just as for growth. The portfolio should now be placed 50 percent in money funds and 50 percent in Treasury notes of one- to three-years' maturity. You're riding out a bear market here, so capital protection is paramount. Also, very few of the bears have lasted as long as three years, so there's really no need for longer-note maturities. You'll likely be back in a stock bull market before that long.

In sum, income investors have two choices of how to deal with stock bull market signals. When stock-generated income is adequate for your projected needs and you can take advantage of the market's growth potential to increase capital for future income production, follow the plan above according to each Model signal. Or, if your income needs are greater, you'll usually find them better met by the bond market and its Model signals. In either case, you should be receiving some capital growth along with the income to store away. And, each plan assiduously protects capital by controlling investment risk along the road.

In fact, I have never seen another investment income plan that offers the combination of good income, capital growth potential, and capital protection that these two do.

Do study the details of them to the point of your comfort. You certainly want to be at ease with the source of your new-found support.

PROTECTING YOUR GAINS

The final matter that needs our attention is a critical one. It's also technical in the sense that it requires studying stock charts to put the most important profit protection device known to investment pros in place. It is the sell stop order, better known, misleadingly, as the stop-loss.

We could spend most of a chapter in explanation and examples of placing stop orders on stocks. There are sufficient permutations of stock price patterns to permit that. However, the basic rules we use are simple enough that we can leave the variations to the times when specific stocks are recommended in my *Low-Risk GROWTH Letter.* You'll have enough information to make your own sell stop decisions if you'll pay close attention to the three examples here.

The single purpose of sell stop orders is to protect capital against surprise developments on individual stocks. They can also be used on market indexes, but may interfere with our Right Market Models' moving average signals. I prefer to use them mainly with individual issues where they can play a real role in guarding capital against market emotion or what we'll call the "somebody knows something" price plunge. (I also urge their use with gold and bonds.)

The first example, Lomas Financial, is a great case in point (Figure 6–10). Note the box in the upper left section. It contains annual price range and earnings for the stock. Note the earnings loss for 1988, during which year the stock had a price range of 22 to 11. But, for 1989 and 1990, Wall Street estimates are for a sharp rebound in those earnings. Things are looking pretty good in the fundamentals since earnings are a key ingredient in stock price movements. The stock was reflecting this up to October 1, 1988, selling around 19 on that date.

The second Lomas chart shows the "somebody knows" problem. Earnings estimates had been *raised* for 1990, but the

FIGURE 6–10
Lomas Financial January 88–June 89*

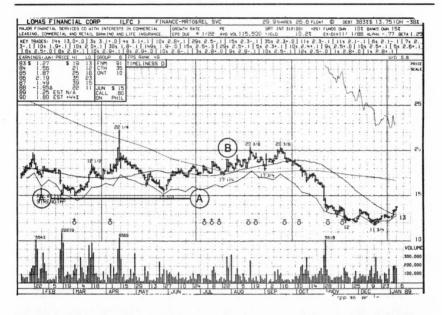

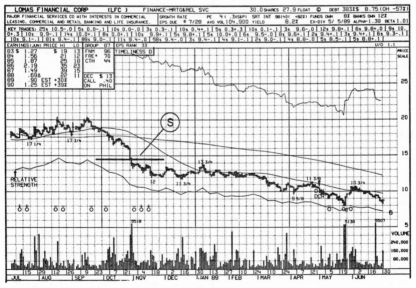

*Source: Courtesy of Daily Graphs, P.O. Box 24933, Los Angeles, CA 90024

stock headed south to 9½. Sell stop orders can do wonders to protect against this sort of contrariness.

Investors should follow these steps in placing their stops. (Traders may well want to use a somewhat different procedure because their stops should be much tighter to the current price. A fine discussion of this technique for traders is in Stan Weinstein's *Secrets of Profiting From Bull and Bear Markets*, published by Dow Jones-Irwin in 1988.)

For investors, we're first looking for a chart condition where over a period of at least three months' time the stock price has bottomed in the same narrow range: Within one point is OK for average priced stocks, within 2–3 percent for higher priced issues. At least *two* bottoms in the range are necessary; having *three* is even better. This occurred with Lomas at about 15¼, shown as line A–A.

Note that this is a condition that exists no matter what price you paid for the stock. For this reason we'll ignore buy prices for now.

The theory behind this is that if the stock has traded in a narrow flat range for a decent period, it shows good buying support there. If the stock then rises and falls back to that area, buyers should be willing to step in at the same area again. Next, investors should give the support line plenty of room in pricing the actual stop. I like to place the stop about a full point below the lowest close in the support area. That would be about 14⅜ as the sell stop *price* for Lomas.

Once the support area is identified, the next step is *timing* the placement of the sell stop order. This is as important as price selection because placing it too soon after the support is identified may get in the way of a trading dip that reveals the support is insufficient, causing a quick stop out. Of course, there's no guarantee this won't occur later, but by following one rule on placement timing your odds of having the support broken on a mere trading dip are lessened. In following the rule, the probability is that any breakdown thereafter will be meaningful, that is, the stock is on its way much lower.

The timing I've found that works best is to establish the stop order *after* the stock has risen above its 200-day moving average for 3 sessions. This usually indicates the stock has sufficient strength and buying interest above the support to avoid a trading range triggering of the stop. With Lomas, this time is shown at point B. That's the chart pattern that says *when* to place the sell stop below the support line A–A. A further point of stop order pricing: Never use a round number for the stop price. Too many investors do place round number orders to buy or sell with the result that the stock easily trades at those numbers. You want your stop to require something more than an easy trade on the specialist's book. Use eighths, preferably just *below* a round number like 15 or 14½, as in the Lomas case.

Also, use daily closes for your stops, rather than intraday prices. Price spikes happen too often during the day to run that risk. By the close, things have usually settled down, unless the move is for real. Note the spike in Lomas at 22¼. That cleared out a lot of buy orders just before the stock fell by 30 percent to near 15.

Finally, *don't* actually place the stop order with your broker. If it's an over-the-counter (OTC) stock, the broker probably won't accept it anyway. And if it's exchange listed, you're letting the specialist (and anyone else who asks for a quote while the stock is trading near your order) know where it stands. I've seen too many cases of a stop getting picked off just by being on the books before a price run contrary to the order. So keep your stop a mental one, based on a closing price only, and set it an eighth of a point below a round number, and you'll have better chances of having the stop do its job properly.

One caveat: Treat the close-only mental stop exactly as if it were entered with a broker, and execute it the following day. Don't second guess it, or you'll find yourself talking to yourself that whole day. When the stop is hit (or pierced) on a close, make the sale the next day, period. No rethinking.

Back to Lomas. The second chart shows what happened to the stop. It was triggered at point S, on big volume, with an order execution the next day at 14¼ or 14⅜. That saved approximately 5 points from the sale to the low, which on 14⅜ amounts to more than ⅓. Since recovery of a 33 percent loss requires a gain of 50 percent, you see the magnitude of the problem you've avoided. Not to mention six months of agonizing

FIGURE 6–11
Wyse Technology January 88 to June 89

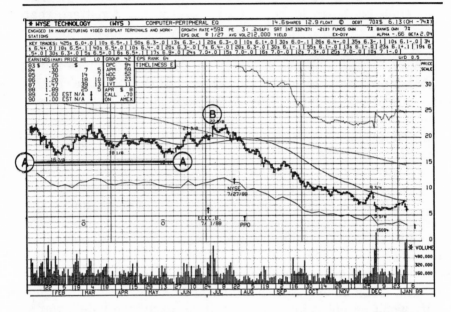

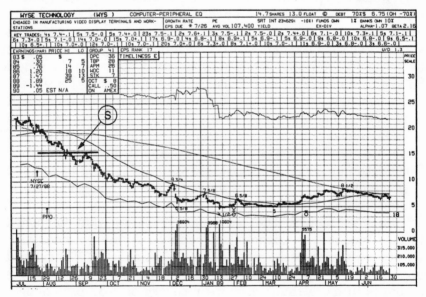

*Source: Courtesy of Daily Graphs, P.O. Box 24933, Los Angeles, CA 90024

over how low it might drop. If you still like the stock later, it can always be rebought and a new stop established under better conditions.

A similar situation seems to have developed with Wyse Technology in Figure 6–11 except that the company had publicly announced its problems with layoffs and negative earnings forecasts. Still, the Street thinks the firm will be profitable next year. The stock doesn't.

Our stop should have been set at about 15⅜, and established in early July 1988 as the stock broke above its 200-day MA. Fortunately, as the second Wyse chart shows, that was about the end of the ball game. The sale would have been made in mid-August, probably at 15 or a bit higher, saving a loss of 10 points or a whopping 66 percent to the low. How long do you think recovery from that might take? In percent, that's a lot to ask!

Interestingly, and contrary to Lomas, Wyse looks like it might have bottomed around a 4¾ close during January through April 1989. If this situation develops satisfactorily and a new buy was made, where should the new sell stop be placed? 3⅞ should be safe, but a more aggressive investor might try 4⅜ close only.

Sure, if the stock was bought, say around 8, a stop just above 4 doesn't sound like a stop loss. More like a create loss. But, if the stock breaks below the support in the mid-4s, we're probably talking bankruptcy here. This means it's a high-risk situation, no matter what. Wouldn't a 40 percent loss still be better than 80 percent, if the stock went to the Chapter Eleven area of about 1½? The management makes no guarantees, as friend Louis Rukeyser likes to point out. But if I were to buy this stock around the 8 level, I'd sure want downside protection with a stop. I'd just make the commitment with an amount of money, 40 percent of which I felt I could lose. See comments at the end of this section about an alternative method of setting this type of stop.

It should be clear by now that the point of setting stops is *not* to avoid losing *any* money, but to sidestep major losses, or to recognize where such a loss might occur so that you can control the amount of money at risk. Frankly, I've stopped using the phrase "stop loss" order. Clearly, these orders might not do that at all. But, I trust you see they can be valuable when used properly.

Hold on. There's another positive to the sell stop, and we can see it on the charts of one of the great growth stocks, Sam Walton's Wal-Mart Stores in Figure 6–12. The idea here (and with any stock that rises in price after purchase) is to raise the stop order as the price progresses. That keeps you in the stock, adding profits, but avoiding significant downturns. After all, Wal-Mart still sells at above 20 times estimated earnings, and sold above 50 times in 1987! It ain't without risk.

This chart pattern is typical of growth stocks, where the base or bottom formation is not a straight line like I've drawn at A–A or C–C. Instead the May 1988 decline to the 26 area, PLUS the move back up above the 200-day MA, constituted a test of the prior 24-plus area. In high-growth stocks, this is typical and about the most you should expect. It's a valid test in any case, as long as the follow-on upswing crosses a solid MA. Some pros like it to go one better by seeing it set a new recovery, or actual, high. Wal-Mart did that at 31.

OK. So we set the first stop at time B, at a level of 24⅞, just below the January–February 1988 low closes at line A–A.

By January 1989, we've identified a potential area to which to raise the stop, C–C. It's contained two tests of the "congestion area" between 28 and 30: one in August, the other in November 1988. On the first chart we still don't have a time at which to place the stop. What's more, the stock seems to be staying above its 200-day MA, so we don't have a crossover of that line as a timing signal.

In such cases, we require a new closing high as the timing point, and one occurred in February 1989 at 34½. That's when we'd set our mental sell stop at a closing price of 28⅞. And, if Sam keeps pushing goods through his shops at his recent 32 percent annual growth rates, we'll hope to keep resetting our stops higher 'til the cows come home.

There is a further point that needs to be made concerning setting the *initial* stop after you buy a stock. Consider the case of Wyse Technology where you're buying the stock around 8 for any sound reason, not just the chart pattern.

The best stop is around the 4 level for reasons noted earlier. But, if you want to take a shorter-term view and not risk a loss from 8 to 4, you can look for a less substantial support area closer to the buy price. In Wyse this would be just under the

FIGURE 6-12
Wal-Mart July 88 to January 89*

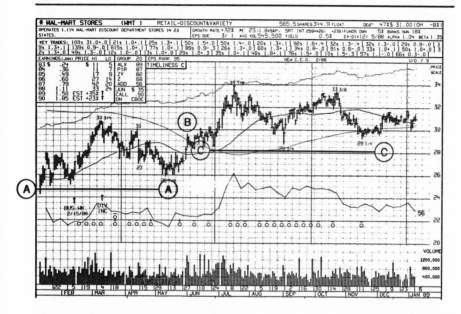

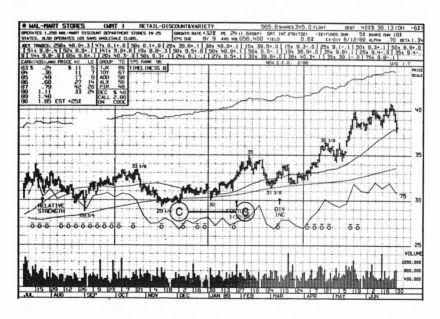

*Source: Daily Graphs, P.O. Box 24933, Los Angeles, CA 90024

April two week support around 6½. A 6⅜, close-only stop could thus be used on the initial buy. This would limit the loss to about 20 percent if triggered. It's a far riskier level at which to place the stop because the support there was just a couple of weeks' trading. But, it has the advantage of creating only a moderate loss if the market goes against you.

This follows one of the best stock trading rules: Be ready to take a small loss and admit an error, rather than let the loss become significant. I know of no better adage in the business, so I'd favor this alternative procedure on an initial buy IF the best stop setting process described earlier creates a loss potential *in excess* of 20 percent, AND at least a *two week* chart support level can be seen within 20 percent, and preferably 10 percent, of your buy price. Use this alternative on the first purchase you make of a stock and only when these two conditions can be met. Don't use it for bonds or gold bullion supports of only a couple of weeks as these markets are about as solid as gossamer.

Summary

The marvelous fact about the stock market is that it offers investors such a wide range of opportunities. One can take a short- or long-term view, play it from a long or short position, use individual stocks or one of more than 1,000 stock mutual funds, and follow technical or fundamental analysis in selection of both market timing and participation vehicles. With the Right Market approach we integrate these choices into one system that has produced a return more than double that of a stock market buy-hold over our two decade-plus test period. And, it has produced gains of over *10 times* that buy-hold when its other markets' signals are counted. It has this potential for the future, too.

However, RMM requires one critical investor attribute—patience. It is a medium- to long-term approach whose success is based on not trying to catch every market swing. If you can utilize this quality, and follow just four market indicators for stocks, odds are high that you'll succeed while taking only moderate investment risk at all times.

The second leg of our three market structure, bonds, uses nearly the same indicators as stocks and, now that it's 35-year bear market has been laid to rest, offers a unique combination of income along with gain potential. It's one market that no investor can now afford to ignore.

CHAPTER 7

BEATING BONDS

"Blessed are the young, for they shall inherit the national debt." —*Herbert Hoover*

President Hoover's quip sounds antiquated today. But the problem is different from his era only because it's gotten drastically worse. In fact, the national debt is so enormous that pundits don't even wisecrack about it anymore. Now it's the *current* deficits, federal and trade, that bear the gibes. And serious worry besides.

Bonds of course, whomever they're issued by, are debt instruments. And funding them today, both their interest and principal amounts, is a heavy expense for the great majority of issuers, due to the volume outstanding. Recent estimates of interest on the federal debt alone are about 25 percent of the annual government budget, and U.S. corporations are spending around 22 percent of their cash flow for debt service. The former is an all-time record, and the latter is a level seen only at recession bottoms. The pair represents a staggering burden to bear if for no other reason than interest must be paid. "When you can't borrow the interest, you're broke," goes the old line. We're getting close.

But, perhaps surprisingly, U.S. government debt quality is still arguably among the best in the world. The presumption remains that its interest and principal will be paid. Never mind that it might be paid with drastically depreciated dollars and/or new taxes. Most everyone presumes it will be paid.

The one aspect of U.S. government bonds, then, that bond buyers worry least about, is their credit risk. This may become a wrongly ignored trepidation, but for now, the assumption we must make is that the government is good for the bucks.

To be sure, credit risk is important for any bond issuer, and it must be addressed in considering most bonds. Market professionals use bond rating services to quantify this element, and that's where the AAA to D bond ratings, or variations on those letters, come into play. For our purposes, though, we want to eliminate as many factors in our bond investment decisions as possible. We'll focus for the moment on U.S. Treasuries for that reason and for their ready marketability.

Bonds are one leg of our three market concept for the simple reason that they represent a pure play on the deflation (or disinflation) economic scenario. In this aspect bonds cover the reverse side of the inflation coin. They perform best in price when inflation rates are perceived to be declining. As noted earlier, the history of the past 40 years shows this has been a rare event. But, longer stretches of modern history, large parts of the 20s and 30s, for example, found bonds performing very well. And the anti-inflation stance in Washington since 1979 has made them important market winners during a large part of the 1980s. They can't be ignored in our concept.

By expecting to periodically use bonds in our program to cover the deflation/disinflation economy, we've implicitly raised the second form of bond risk: inflation. No other category of investments is as negatively sensitive to real and perceived inflation problems as bonds. Shortly we'll address a third important bond danger—market or interest rate risk. Recognizing both these risks leads us directly to the most accurate indicators we can use to time purchases and sales in the bond market.

INFLATION RISK

To ensure that we're on the same wavelength here, let's recall why inflation is a risk to bond prices.

Let's take a 10-year Treasury bond with an 8 percent interest coupon at a price of $1,000. And let's assume a 7 percent average annual inflation rate over the 10 years to the bond's maturity. When the Treasury pays off that bond's principal of $1,000, the cash will buy something less than one-half of what $1,000 bought upon the bond's issuance. Seven percent annual inflation cuts capital's purchasing power by 50 percent in just over 10 years.

So who would want to buy that bond if the Treasury offered it? Not many investors, if they expected to hold it to maturity and anticipated that 7 percent average inflation rate for the duration. The guaranteed return of their $1,000 in 10 years is a promise they'd just as soon avoid if it would buy only $500 worth of this year's goods and services. But, with one caveat: if the interest rate paid on their bond compensated for the inflation, and the interest could be compounded at the inflation rate or more each year, the net return might be adequate. So, a 10–10 ½ percent coupon might sell the bond if a 10 percent compounding vehicle could be found, since 3 percent above the estimated inflation rate is in the neighborhood of the true cost of money.

But the real problem is that no one can forecast an inflation rate that far ahead. The one constant fact about inflation is that it varies. It never remains the same for an extended period. Given the variables, then, a 10 percent interest rate is probably too low in this scenario. Eleven or twelve percent might be more like it, depending on whether the inflation rate was rising or falling at the time of the offering.

So, the effect of inflation on the bond market is a powerful one. Bonds must compensate for it by demanding higher interest rates. That means lower prices for all bonds outstanding. This is the only way to make up for inflation's haircut on bond principal.

This clearly tells us that one or more of our bond market indicators must address inflation rate changes.

INTEREST RATE RISK

A close corollary to inflation risk is that arising from interest rate changes that may not be related to inflation. Even though most of the rate changes that the Federal Reserve Board engineers are connected to its perception of the inflation danger, others need not be. A rise in rates to make the dollar more attractive to foreign buyers is one example. A lowering of rates to stimulate a slumping economy is another. There may be inflation inputs to such changes, naturally, but the primary reason for a given rate change can be other than inflation.

The effect of the rate change on the bond market will be the same no matter the reason for it, however. Arithmetic demands that rising rates cause lower bond prices, and vice versa. And, that the rate changes will have a more pronounced effect on longer-term bonds than on short.

A handy table to assess this degree of price change by maturity says that for each one percentage point change in *yield* on an 8 percent debt instrument selling at par (a price of $1,000 face amount), we'll get approximately the following change in *price*:

0.9 percent on a one-year bill
6.5 percent on a 10-year note
10 percent on a 30-year bond

Thus, if the Fed forces a full percentage point change in the overnight borrowing market it directly controls—the federal funds market—all other things being equal, the above price changes will quickly ripple through the bill, note, and bond markets.

"All other things" are rarely equal, of course, and the Fed usually does not make that great a change in market rates at a given time. One-half point changes are more common, as with the 1987–89 hikes in the Fed's basic lending rate, the discount rate. And price changes of about half the above amounts did move quickly through the maturity structure in each case. In fact, even larger price changes occurred, partially prior to and after each rate increase, because the market sniffed further rate changes to come. The bond market is nothing if not paranoid.

The net of this is that in order to effectively time bond market purchases a sound indicator of the direction the Fed is leaning on its interest rate changes is critical. Fortunately, we have one in the STIR Index, as previously discussed.

We now see at least two indicators that tend to forecast bond price action are necessary to cover both inflation trend changes and Fed interest rate action that may be independent of inflation factors. Our SIMPL indicator types fit again. Indeed, the "M" is also needed, so, a trend change indicator for bond *prices* themselves also makes sense. A well-proven moving average should work to cover bond market paranoia.

THE INDICATOR COMBINATION

After our previous extensive discussion of the basic indicator types and specific formats for four of them in Scoring in Stocks, we can see that they should work neatly for bonds, too. The track record in Figure 7–1 shows that the Weighted CPI and STIR Index called the bond market on a simple 1–2 basis, except for 1980 and 1987.

All but one combination was a winner, but the 1980 loss of about 10 percent was modest compared to the compound total return of over 277 percent.

From the record, we see that a moving average did not play a role in bond market transactions until 1987. That's because market movements through it occurred *after* other signals in the prior 20 years. The two indicators caught the trends sufficiently well. But, 1987 warns us to pay more attention to the MA concept with bonds in the future.

Figure 7–2 shows how well a 15-month (65-week) moving average has worked with the S&P Long-Term Government Bond Index over the past 20 years. As with stocks, we use a filter, 3 percent in this case, to avoid whipsaws. That modest addition took care of the 1968 and 1982 apparent whipsaw crossovers, plus the almost unnoticeable ones on the chart in 1973 and 1980.

We can now combine these indicators into our Bond Market Model. As with any medium-term indicators, they won't achieve

FIGURE 7–1
W.CPI and STIR Bond Signals, 1968–1988[a]

Jan.	1968	Rising Consumer Prices:	Sell bonds
Jun.	1970	Falling Consumer Prices:	Buy bonds
Oct.	1972	Rising W.CPI:	Sell bonds (profit)
Feb.	1975	Falling W.CPI:	Buy bonds
Jun.	1977	Rising STIR:	Sell bonds (profit)
Aug.	1980	Falling W.CPI:	Buy bonds
Nov.	1980	Rising STIR:	Sell bonds (loss)
Oct.	1981	Falling STIR:	Buy bonds
Sept.	1983	Rising W.CPI:	Sell bonds (profit)
Dec.	1984	Falling W.CPI:	Buy bonds
Apr.	1987	Market MA:	Sell bonds (profit)

[a]Note that weighted CPI was first available in 1972. A moving average of the CPI itself was used prior to that.

FIGURE 7–2
S&P LT Bonds, 1967-77

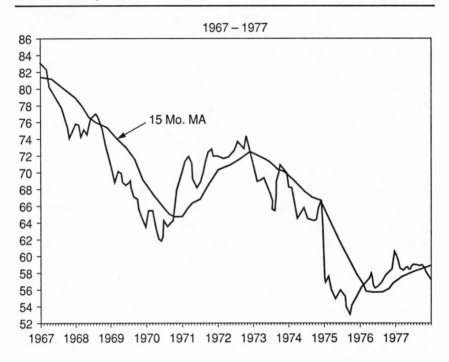

1967 – 1977

the optimum buy or sell price in every case. That's why they're medium-term in outlook. They snip off the last bit of the bottoms and peaks in order to always catch the major part of the move. Our back-tested Bond Model has generated a correct signal for all but one major long-term bond move for two decades. It did better than a bond buy-hold over the period by some 60 percent. Our previous discussion suggests there's strong reason to believe it will perform similarly in the future.

THE BOND MODEL RULES

1. The first Model indicator to generate a signal by moving through its key MA is an *alert* to an important turn in bond prices. It can come from any one of the three indicators: STIR, Weighted CPI or its price index MA.

FIGURE 7–2—*Continued*
S&P LT Bonds, 1978-88*

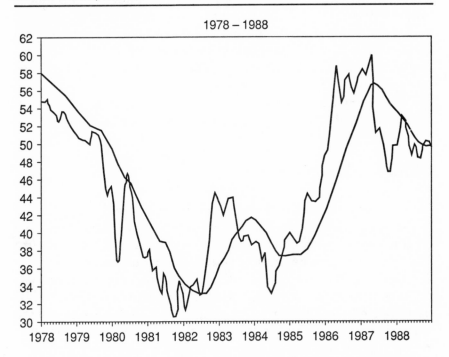

2. When a second indicator gives a signal in the same direction as the first, (a Model + 2 reading), a bond buy or sell signal is triggered. Buy long-term bonds or bond funds with maximum capital allowed by asset allocation rules in Chapter 10. A third signal is the icing.

3. On the downside, when the Model falls from + 3 to + 2, *sell* one-half your long-term bond position. Note that MA crossovers must be more than superficial: On the basis shown, the month's average bond price should move at least 3 percent through the MA.

4. Whenever the model reverts to only a + 1 or zero reading, investors should sell out of long-term bonds entirely.

Notice that in 1980, the opposite STIR signals in May and November created a sale in November that returned the

---

*Source: Standard & Poor Corp., New York, and Kinsman & Associates.

weighted CPI signal in August to an alert. This lasted until the STIR buy signal in October 1981 which gave the +2 Model reading necessary for another buy.

With the indicators used in this manner we address all three forms of bond market movements: inflation risk, the Fed's moves on rates that aren't inflation prompted, and market moves alone.

The final Bond Model buy-sell combinations are shown in Figure 7–3 with results summarized below the table.

REAL TIME EXAMPLES

Let's see how the Bond Model would have triggered actions in a real-time sequence. In Figure 7–4, we have the Model readings on the T-bond *yield* chart, based on the transactions in Figure 7–3. The sequence beginning in 1981 is the easiest to see.

Growth investors were out of the long-term bond market in November 1980, with a Model reading of +1. Both the STIR (see Figure 6–5 in the previous chapter) and MA crossover were negative, and you can see from the chart that bond yields were rising steeply, meaning prices were falling sharply.

In October 1981, STIR turned positive, giving the Model a +2 reading and signaling that the bond portion of the portfolio should be at maximum exposure to bonds. This means 100 percent invested in long Treasuries or equivalent bond funds, IF there is no other bull market underway at the time. (See Asset Allocation rules in Chapter 10.)

The following August, the bond market moved above its long-term MA, giving us a +3 Model level. The chart shows this was followed by the maximum price rise (yield decline) in two decades. By June 1983, STIR reverted to a negative, giving the Model a +2 mark. This was a *first sell* by our rules, and it came almost precisely at the bond price high and yield low. One-half of the long-term bond portfolio should have been switched to a money market fund. (Again note that our Figure 7–2 track record doesn't give credit for this trade, even though it was 2 points higher than the "sell all" of July 1983.) The latter occurred with the MA break of that month, leaving the

FIGURE 7–3
Complete Bond Model Signals/Results 1970–1989

(Based on S&P Long-Term Bond Index average price in month data reported) Note that weighted CPI was not available until 1972.

March 1970	STIR positive.
October 1970	MA positive, Model +2: Buy @ 64.85. Interest rate: 7.0%.
August 1972	STIR negative, Model +1: Sell @ 74.27: Gain 14.5%. Interest earnings 12.9% in 22 months.
October 1972	W.CPI negative, Model 0.
January 1973	MA negative, Model 0.
October 1974	STIR positive, Model +1.
February 1975	W.CPI positive, Model +2: Buy @ 57.92. Interest rate: 7.8%.
January 1976	MA positive, Model +3.
March 1977	W.CPI negative, Model +2: Sell 1/2 @ 58.36.
May 1977	STIR negative, Model +1: Sell all @ 58.43: Gain 1.0%. Interest earnings 17.6% in 27 months.
October 1977	MA negative, Model 0.
May 1980	STIR positive, Model +1.
August 1980	W.CPI positive, Model +2: Buy @ 41.86. Interest rate: 11.5.%
November 1980	STIR negative, Model +1: Sell all @ 37.62: Loss 10.1%. Interest earnings 2.9% in 3 months.
October 1981	STIR positive, Model +2: Buy @ 30.72. Interest rate: 14.6.%
August 1982	MA positive, Model +3.
June 1983	STIR negative, Model +2: Sell 1/2 @ 42.26.
July 1983	MA negative, Model +1: Sell all @ 40.56. Gain 32.0%. Interest earnings 25.5% in 21 months.
September 1983	W.CPI negative, Model 0.
October 1984	MA positive, Model +1 and STIR positive, Model +2: Buy @ 38.22. Interest rate 11.9%.
December 1984	W.CPI positive, Model +3.
February 1987	W.CPI negative, Model +2: Sell 1/2 @ 58.16.
April 1987	MA negative, Model +1: Sell all @ 54.01. Gain 41.1%. Interest earnings 29.8% in 30 months.
May 1987	STIR negative, Model 0.
January 1988	W.CPI positive, Model +1.
August 1988	W.CPI negative, Model 0.
January 1989	W.CPI positive, Model +1.
April 1989	W.CPI negative, Model 0.

Note: The following summary excludes partial position sales for ease of understanding. It assumes all sales were made on the final sale date and combines gains with interest for total return.

Totals:	1970-1972:	+27.4%
	1974-1977:	+18.6%
	1980:	(7.2)%
	1981-1983:	+57.5%
	1984-1987:	+70.9%
Compound Gain		277.4%

Despite being invested only 44% of the 20 years discussed, the compound return per year for the period was 5.3%. No interest was calculated as earned on cash balances. The totals compare to a buy and hold strategy from October 1970 to April 1987 of *minus* 16.7 percent on capital, plus interest of 117.2 percent for a net return of 100.5 percent for the entire period. This annual return was thus a dismal less than one percent compounded. Our Model signals produced nearly three times these results.

FIGURE 7–4
Bond Model Signals on 30-Year Treasury Bond Yields*

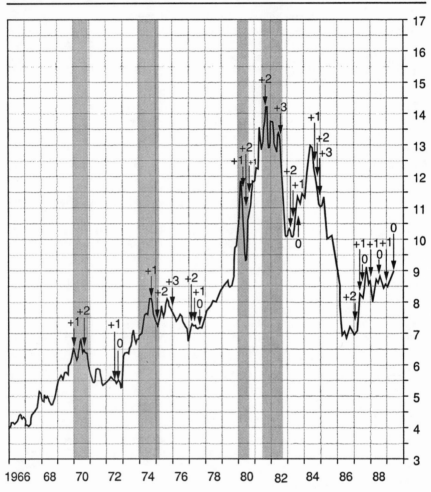

Model at +1, and our position 100 percent in a money fund.
The Model did not signal a return to the long bond market until
November the following year when it was done at an average
price a bit below the previous exit price.

The Model missed the fast turnaround at the bond yield
highs in mid-1984, alright, but it still captured a fine 70.9

---

*Source: the Business Picture, op. cit., Chapter 2.

percent *total return* in the following 2 ½ years. That was the best of the entire period shown.

This timing sequence in the 1984 to 1987 period is the best example of how our Model performs in real time. It gave up the yield spike of about 2 percentage points in summer 1984 because it is designed to not be fooled by temporary trends that can easily amount to this much. But it caught the major move of the period and provided an outstanding return for its investors.

If you are an impatient investor, or are trying to snare every move of almost any size, forget this Method. It won't do that for you. But if you want to get aboard the truly major profit moves and ignore the modest ones, RMM and the specific Bond Model rules are designed for exactly that.

Unless the bond market begins to pay more attention to factors other than Fed intervention and inflation rate gyrations (a most unlikely probability due to the nature of the U.S. financial system and of bonds themselves) we have a Right Market approach to bonds that should continue to function well. Theory and practice mesh over a period of 5 cycles covering 18 years. The number of cycles is less than optimal, but the strength of the theory backing the indicators is sufficient to compensate for it. Indeed, we've beaten bonds during one of their roughest eras in the century, 1972–1987. And RMM even came out with a positive 140.2 percent total return through the complete bear market segment, 1972–1980.

SENTIMENT FINE TUNING

Our sentiment measure, the Bullish Consensus (BC) of bond futures traders, can now be brought to the fore. Recall that it's used as a trade refining technique, not a Model indicator, in the same way it's used with stocks. We want it to permit selling into strong positive opinion and buying into negative, but if that isn't available at the time of the Model signal we'll make the trade with a two-week trend in these directions.

The bond BC first became available in September 1980. The bullish percentages shown are for the sequential weeks of the month immediately following the Model buy or sell signals.

September 1980 BC percentages: 50, 49, 39, 34, 60. Buy on weakness at 39 percent.

November 1980: 39, 43, 60, 56. Sell on strength at 60 percent.

October 1981: 44, 60, 48, 32, 59. Buy on weakness at 32 percent.

July 1983: 36, 31, 35, 44, 29. Sell on strength at 44 percent.

November 1984: 79, 65, 73, 81, 59. Buy on weakness reversal at 73 percent. (Prior 12-month high was 84 percent, so record high rule not triggered.)

April 1987: 27, 18, 29, 30, 34. Sell on 2-week strength at 30 percent.

As with stocks, the Bullish Consensus provides the desired sell-strength, buy-weakness concept, in most cases. It can't guarantee the best price over the time frame, but it does allow us to take advantage of its tendency to parallel market trends.

BOND VEHICLES

Growth investors have many choices of bond vehicles that will fully participate in our Right Market Method. The most obvious first alternative is between taxable and tax-exempt bonds. Here the choice is a personal one based on your tax bracket, and is probably a choice you've already made. My suggestion is that if you do invest for tax exempt income that you use long-term municipal bonds that carry one of the two highest ratings in your state: AAA or AA. This may not generate the highest possible income, in that lower rated issues yield more. But, when investing for growth, this is a condition that's well traded off for peace of mind in reduced credit risk. By long-term I mean those maturities in excess of 20 years. When the Bond Model signals a confirmed buy, it's these issues that will provide the biggest bang for the buck.

A second criterion for municipals is that they either have no call provision, or that the call be at least three years away from date of purchase. It's unlikely that a bond bull market will last that long, at least it hasn't anytime in the past 40 years, so insisting on call protection past three years appears unnecessary. But three years should still be the minimum call protection to avoid any concern about having your bond capital gains taken away during a bull market by a premature call.

Finally, there are many zero coupon municipal issues available, and these provide the greatest capital gain potential. The absence of a coupon gives zeros far greater price volatility than standard munis of a given maturity. Growth investors willing to accept the greater volatility should consider muni zeros when the Bond Model says buy. Again, use the longest maturities available.

Municipal bond mutual funds are also widely available and are perfectly appropriate for RMM bond signals. Stay with those issued for your state, if it's a relatively high tax area and muni funds do concentrate in it. Also, ensure that the fund is a long-term muni fund, as there are many short-term funds available, but they will only reduce the gain potential for a given long-term bond market rise. The large no-load fund families all have several state and national tax-exempt bond funds. See next page and Appendix.

The alternatives to munis for taxable bond investors are either corporates or Treasuries, and my preference is again to stay with the highest quality, which means Treasuries. Why deal with a potential credit risk problem in selecting corporates, even the highest rated? And why bother about call protection, something that Treasuries avoid by being noncallable?

In these days of corporate takeovers, there's a new negative for company bonds on Wall Street that's been dubbed *event risk*. It's what happened to RJR Nabisco bonds when the raid started and their quality rating was sliced from single A in a two-level cut to BB, virtually overnight. Prices fell nearly 20 percent to compensate for the overwhelming added debt the firm was expected to acquire. Same story with the Time, Inc. and Warner Communications bonds in spring of 1989.

So again, when growth is "paramount," the extra yield in corporates rarely makes sense unless you're an experienced junk valuer. Stay with Treasuries, at least until bond protection groups get an adequate immunity from this event risk for all corporate bonds—they're working on it.

Incidentally, corporate bond mutual funds are satisfactory holdings for average investors, in my opinion, but only if their own quality rating is high or the average holdings' maturity is short, three to five years. Their diversification wins out.

The choice among other vehicles is again wide. But it's simple. Long-term Treasury bond funds (no-load) are issued by all the major mutual fund families, including Vanguard, T. Rowe Price, Fidelity, Benham, Twentieth Century, Federated and Scudder, to name the best known. At this writing, Benham and Scudder had zero coupon funds, which, as with muni zeros, provide the greatest volatility and gain potential.

If you wish to buy long Treasuries individually, any of the longest maturities listed will do for maximum capital growth, as will zero coupon issues. In both cases, however, be aware that purchases under about $100,000 par value will be treated by the market as very small fry, subject to wider spreads between bid and offer and not immodest commissions. No-load Treasury mutual funds will probably be the best vehicle for the average investor.

Don't forget the Government National Mortgage Association (GNMA) certificates and government agency bonds. These often provide higher income with virtually all the advantages of Treasuries. Again, income is not the main reason in buying for growth, but if you can improve on it without a disadvantage tradeoff, why not consider it? Be aware, though, that GNMA certificates and those held in mutual funds don't have an average life much more than 12–15 years, which means their volatility is less than long Treasuries in the 30-year maturity range. That's OK, if your decision is to invest with less than maximum volatility.

A few words should be said here about managing bond portfolios with the Right Market Method, such as those held for pension, profit sharing, and other fiduciary sponsors. With no other securities are exact and detailed decisions about sponsor's goals, constraints, and other terms as important as they are with bonds. That's basically because Aunt Tillie's money is with such plans and amateur fiddling with the bundle is frowned upon.

Since it appears that a part of the current state of the bond portfolio management art is determination of performance adequacy through what's known as a "baseline portfolio" (a theoretical model of the exact portfolio demanded by the plan's goals and objectives), our Bond Model and rules should be used in this management only when the baseline permits extensive shifting of risk levels. In short, don't take on the risk of long-term bonds and especially their zero-coupon equivalents if your plan's goals/constraints require a three- to five-year portfolio duration or similar risk control. It isn't that long-term bonds have such vastly greater risks than, say stocks, but plan sponsors tend to think they do when you leap parameters and lose upon landing.*

FOR INCOME INVESTORS ONLY

Investors who need maximum income from their investments at all times should obviously follow different investment rules than those looking for capital growth. Following is a specific bond plan for income investors only.

The bond market provides obvious vehicles for income investing, both in the taxable and tax-exempt categories. It also offers a range of specific maturities and mutual funds with differing maturity ranges that allow investors to either avoid or accept the increased capital risk of longer maturities. These alternatives, plus the ubiquitous money market funds, permit investors to follow a sound general rule for maximizing income and capital appreciation at any point in the bond market bull and bear cycles. Investors never need be out of the fixed income market, a handy condition if you need the income every month or quarter. Instead, they need only to adjust portfolio maturity structure to changing bond market conditions. This will also automatically reduce both interest rate and inflation risks, if done correctly. Credit risk is best handled by owning only U.S. government or AA or better rated municipal bonds, perhaps in mutual funds, at all times.

1. Income investors should buy bonds or bond mutual funds with maturities longer than about five years *only* when the Bond Model is favorable, a +2 reading. Specifically, at that buy signal, shift 75 percent of your portfolio into the longest-term U.S. Treasury, or AA corporate/muni bonds, or long-term

---

* If you'd like to get into this topic, the reprint of Martin L. Leibowitz' 1980 article "Trends in Bond Portfolio Management" in Ellis and Vertin's *Classics: An Investor's Anthology* Dow Jones-Irwin, 1989, pp. 715–728, will get you nicely started.

bond funds. This will maximize both yield and capital growth potential when the bond market is offering good prospects for each.

The choice between bond funds and individual bonds is principally a matter of convenience and capital available. The more you want of the former and the less on hand of the latter, the more you should lean toward bond funds. See the appendix for a list of recommended no-load bond funds as of spring 1989. For more recommendations, see my current *Low-Risk GROWTH Letter.*

2. The balance of the portfolio that's not shifted to long-term bond issues, 25 percent, should be held in money market funds and shorter-term bonds or funds for capital protection in the unlikely event of a quick reversal of the bond buy signal or a 1980 style downturn. Yes, Virginia, this will dilute your maximum returns, but it *is* prudent for most income investors.

3. Hold this structure until a bond *sell* signal is flashed at a Model reading change from +2 to +1. Then an additional 50 percent of the portfolio should be shifted to a money market fund, with the balance placed in notes with maturities no longer than *three years.* These latter purchases should be made on market price weakness only. The maturity maximum is set to reduce price volatility as bond prices decline. They also provide fixed capital availability dates while assuring a known income stream.

This position can then be held until *one* of the Bond Model's indicators next turns favorable, *after* the Model reading drops to zero. At this time, buy select additional T-note or CD maturities up to about 5 years, with 25 percent of portfolio. Again, these buys should be made on price weakness. If the Model has not dropped to a zero reading prior to the +1, as occurred in 1980–81, there's no need to take this step. Stay with the position in paragraph 3 above, which isn't much different from this one, anyway.

The next portfolio change will then occur upon the full bond buy signal, as cited first above.

That's all there is to it.

Do study these rules and the bond indicators until you're comfortable in relying on them. This method of income investing in bonds can be simple to follow and can provide excellent income with low-risk capital appreciation. But it won't do the job for you unless you're able to trust it. Frankly, with the facts and back tests we've discussed, that shouldn't be a difficult goal.

The other side of the bond picture is that of gold. If bonds despise inflation accelerations, gold usually loves it. But, in recent years, this hasn't always been the case. We'll see why, next.

CHAPTER 8

HOW TO GLITTER IN GOLD

Try to save money. Someday it may be valuable again.—
  Anonymous

As we saw in Chapter 2, the gold mining stocks sector provided far and away the best total return of our three markets over the 40 years through 1987. Gains in the "hindsight" gold mining stock bull markets were so much greater than those of bull markets in the S&P Composite Index that the latter looked like a candidate for under-performer of the century.

Of course, the period included the greatest gold bull market of the century, 1968–80, where bullion alone soared to *25 times* its 1968 fixed price of $35 per ounce. And, gold mining stocks are notoriously volatile, which not only provided excess returns during each bull phase, but also created deep bear canyons in which the accurate market timer could rebuy at depressed prices for the next bull run. Double bounces for the price of one, as it were.

Hindsight is, of course, the most wonderful attribute in the investment world. Being able to say what one would have done IF one caught all those tops and bottoms is a delicious armchair pastime. Being able to even come close in real time, as Chaper 3 indicated, is a far more sobering experience. This is especially true in the gold mining stocks because the penalty for even small timing errors is notably high. It's like the poster photo of an old biplane caught suspended in a large, bare tree and captioned, "Flight can be an exciting and meaningful experience, but it's not very forgiving of errors." Gold mining stock traders quickly grasp the meaning of "not very forgiving."

MOST RECENT BEGINNINGS

So much for the warning. How then do we locate the correct gold market buy and sell points with minimum timing errors?

We have a natural starting point during the era in which gold first recaught wide attention in the United States, following the 1934 private holding ban by the government; 1968 was the year of the first major unraveling of the postwar fixed currency exchange system known as the Bretton Woods Agreement. It occurred in the wake of the November 1967 devaluation of the pound sterling, an event that set up the gold crisis of February–March 1968.

It was during the financial press' flurry over that crisis that the American investing public reawakened to gold's potential. This happened coincidentally with the most serious surge in consumer prices since the relaxation of wage and price controls in 1946. It was also the time of great expansion in the volume of gold traded worldwide. So 1968 marks a significant turn in the world's inflation awareness, and with it a need to invest in inflation protection vehicles. A good year, in short, in which to start a search for indicators of bull trends in the most liquid inflation hedge of all, gold, and its related equities.

WHICH INDICATORS?

The first question must be, how well does the inflation rate function as a practical gold price forecaster? Investment professionals have devised a number of indicators (some good, many inadequate) of the trend in inflation rates as precursors to gold price moves. Probably the best of these has been the Leading Index of Inflation (LII) developed at the Columbia Graduate School of Business and now published monthly by that institution's Center for International Business Cycle Research. Its recent track record versus the Consumer Price Index is shown in Figure 8–1. The two graphs' correlation, with an appropriate lag in the CPI, is clearly excellent.

The problem with using this measure *alone* to time gold buys and sells is shown in Figure 8–2, where the LII/CPI is plotted against the S&P Gold Mining Stock Index. Those stocks have been on several occasions better forecasters of inflation than the LII is. Check out the chart: The mining stocks rose along with LII and ahead of the smoothed CPI in 1972. LII was then early in topping in 1974, while inflation and the stocks accelerated to late in the year.

FIGURE 8–1
Leading Index of Inflation and CPI Inflation Rate, 1972-89

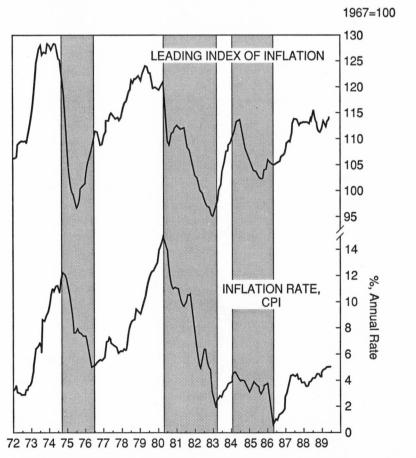

Shaded areas are periods of disinflation, based upon the six-month smoothed growth rates in the consumer price index for all consumers (shown above.)
    Source: Courtesy of Center for International Business Cycle Research, Columbia University.

FIGURE 8–2
S&P Gold Mining Stock Index 1972-88

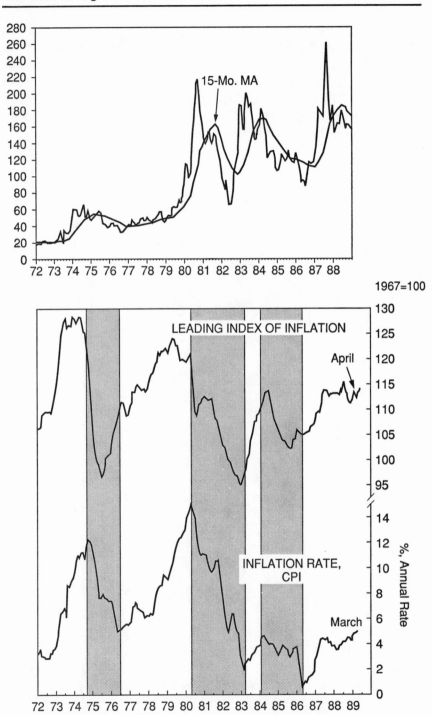

LII then bottomed and turned up in mid-1975, followed by the CPI and mining stocks in mid-1976. So far, LII has been a rather long-lead indicator. LII then topped at the beginning of 1979, almost 18 months before the CPI and mining stocks. That's a long, long lead.

LII bottomed and turned up in 1982, just ahead of the CPI, but the mining stocks took off in August 1982. This was because the gold boom of 1982 was a reaction to the international debt crisis that summer, not to inflation. Reminder: Gold is not always an inflation animal.

Continuing to reflect this situation, now easing, the mining stocks topped in early 1983 while inflation was still rising. The precious yellow had overrun its inflation-price connection, whatever it was, and was now attempting to get back into line. After the late spike in the gold stocks in early 1984, it appears the process was complete and gold again became more of an inflation animal.

LII did another early lead on both gold stocks and the CPI with its bottom in 1985, followed by the other two in early 1986. However, the sharp plunge in the mining stocks in late 1987 was not forecast by LII, although the smoothed CPI did call it.

Most recently in 1989, the mining stocks declined in the face of rises in both the CPI and LII until late spring, when all three moved lower.

In sum, both the LII and a smoothed CPI (six months average in the case plotted), are decent forecasters of trends in the mining stocks on a long lead and roughly coincident basis, respectively, WHEN GOLD IS INFLATION-ORIENTED. But other factors than inflation move the gold price, and must be addressed. We can skip sudden world crisis as not being sufficiently predictable on any regular basis to relate to an indicator. They've been short-term in effect, anyway.

ENTER THE DOLLAR

The international aspect of gold trading is a fact that leads us to another appropriate idea. Gold is, in one view of it, simply another foreign currency. It's traded as an alternative to the U.S. dollar as a refuge in crises and traded like other key foreign currencies during strong dollar periods, when it tends to decline. This suggests an inverse relationship between the U.S. dollar and gold.

Comparing the charts of gold bullion and the Federal Reserve Board (FRB) U.S. Dollar Index in Figure 8–3, we see the relationship in general terms. The FRB Dollar Index is not refined sufficiently here to make the Index itself a gold price

FIGURE 8–3
Federal Reserve Board Dollar Index vs. Gold Bullion Price, 1966–1989

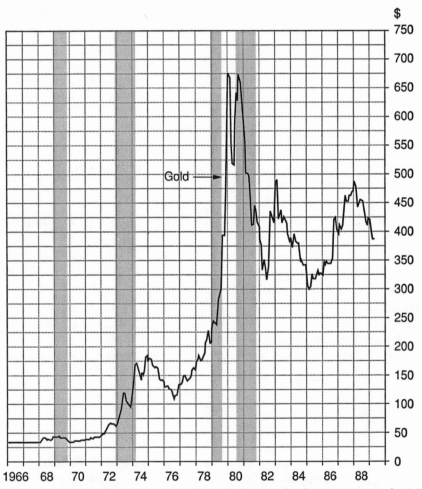

Monthly averages of daily prices from Handy & Harman. London prices are used prior to 1970. Recession periods are shaded. Graph is based on data through March 1989.

Source: Courtesy of *The Business Picture.*, op. cit., Chapter 2.

FIGURE 8–3:—Continued

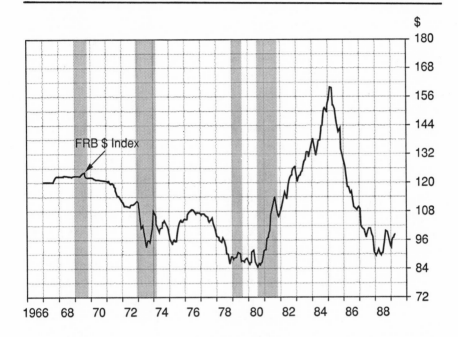

forecaster, but you can see the broad mirror image pattern between it and bullion.

This suggests that the LII, smoothed CPI and the dollar are all forecasters of the gold price, but in somewhat differing ways. The question is, can a way be found to combine them so that we create crosschecks of one another that are useful versus either gold bullion or the gold mining stocks? As you might suppose, the answer is yes.

I must point out to readers of my earlier book, *Low Risk Profits in High Risk Times*, and the original published summary of this book, both of which dealt in part with gold, that the Golden Gates Series of inflation indicators I used successfully with the gold market for many years, simply has too much emphasis on inflation for the market's current focus. Even late in the great inflation era of the 1970s, the dollar became a viable factor in the gold market, but tracking it wasn't necessary because inflation trends overshadowed it. Now, it can't be ignored.

An additional reason for including, and indeed heavily weighting, the dollar factor is that it is a highly sophisticated market. Every major bank and government in the world deals in the foreign currency market, and with the dollar the reserve currency for the world, they must trade in dollars as part of that market. This tends to make the foreign exchange market less subject to flights of fancy or institutional panics than any of our other key markets. And when important trends in it get truly underway, they tend to last for years, not weeks or days. This brings stability to our gold forecasting effort.

The dollar trend's first true reflection in the gold price appears, from Figure 8–3, to show up in late 1976, when its downtrend coincided with the major rise in gold prices then getting underway. The dollar's bottoming in 1980, run to 1985, and plunge to early 1988, run counter to the major trends in gold.

From extensive computer modeling of the interaction between the inflation indicators and the dollar after 1976, we find that the dollar now paints the big picture for gold, but that inflation concerns can affect it, just as international crises can. This concept forms the basis for our revised Gold Model. The Model operates by weighting the FRB Dollar Index slightly more than the CPI and LII *combined*, while a gold price move through *both* its short- and long-term moving averages, as in 1982-83, outweighs all. A short-term MA is used along with the Bullish Consensus of gold futures traders for timing actual trades.

Figure 8–4 on p. 134 is the complete record of the original Golden Gates Series signals sent by the CPI and LII starting in 1967, with the revision to include the FRB Dollar Index at its first signal in 1977. The signals are shown for two price series, gold bullion until Comex futures prices were available in 1976, and the S&P Gold Mining Stock Index. Clearly, the record is outstanding, even if the FRB Dollar Index has generated too few signals to be statistically significant.

The CPI and LII are tracked on a year-over-year percentage change basis with a minimum four-month trend in the same direction required to generate a signal. Rises in inflation indicators are bullish for gold.

The FRB Dollar is measured against its nine-month moving average with a crossover to the upside signaling a negative for gold, and vice versa.

Next, we need action confirmations in order to ensure that the market is awake to the inflation and dollar trends signaled. Here, I've found one that's functioned best throughout the entire 20-year period because it has taken into account gold's own forecasting ability: a price change in the gold market versus a moving average. A short-term MA of six weeks (30 trading days) has been adequate to smooth out the "noise," although a long-term MA of 65 weeks has acted as a second confirmation.

As noted, these two MAs can also act as a shorter-term trading signal as they did in 1982-83, when gold exploded on fears of a world banking collapse with an inflation pickup nowhere to be found until mid-1983. A gold price move up through both MAs in a single month acted as a buy signal in August 1982, while a similar down move generated a sell signal in August 1983. This gives us an added check on gold price action even when its most predictable driving forces are not accelerating. It's also an exception to our long-term buy/sell approach and should therefore only be used by those investors who can stand the volatility and in-out potential this implies.

SENTIMENT

Market Vane's Bullish Consensus survey again performs as a transaction fine tuner with gold. It was first published in 1983, so it doesn't offer a long record to test its accuracy. But the patterns seen for the BC with stocks and bonds are here as well, and as it functions in exactly the same way, it should to provide a sound determination of just how bullish gold futures market participants are. We can then go against them.

The two periods during which the gold BC was available and we had transactions signalled were:

1. April 1985, with weekly bullish readings of 60, 62, 68, 60, and 56 percent. This was an FRB buy signal, so we'd want to act during sentiment weakness. The first two-week downtrend occurred in the last week of April at 56 percent bulls. The buying price that Friday is shown in Figure 8–4.

FIGURE 8–4
Gold Market Signals (all signals are in month data reported)

Date	Signal		Bullion/Comex	SP Gold stocks
September 1967	CPI positive			
October 1967	LII positive:	Buy	$35	15.70
May 1970	CPI negative:			
June 1970	LII negative:	Sell	$35.66	18.56
		Gains:	1.9%	18.2%
June 1971	LII positive:			
October 1972	CPI positive:	Buy	$65.13	20.43
October 1973	LII negative			
March 1975	CPI negative	Sell	$178.29	58.54
		Gains:	173.7%	186.5%
November 1975	LII positive			
October 1976	CPI positive:	Buy	$116.70	36.15
Revision				
March 1977	FRB Index Positive			
November 1979	LII negative			
March 1980	FRB Index negative:	Sell	$549.12	115.5
		Gains:	370.5%	219.5%
May 1980	FRB Index positive:	Buy	$518.24	111.0
August 1980	CPI negative			
November 1980	FRB Index negative:	Sell	$620.40	197.7
		Gains:	19.7%	78.1%
August 1982	Both MAs	Buy	$386.50	79.9
August 1983	Both MAs	Sell	$418.20	195.2
		Gains:	8.2%	144.32%
January 1984	CPI positive			
April 1984	LII negative			
December 1984	CPI negative			
April 1985	FRB Index positive:	Buy	$323.00	134.1
November 1985	LII positive (strong buy)			
February 1986	CPI positive (strong buy)			
June 1986	CPI negative			
May 1987	CPI positive			
November 1987	LII negative			
June 1988	FRB Index negative:	Sell@	$454.50	187.3
		Gains:	40.7%	39.7%

Compound Gains: 6,476.5% for gold stocks
2,291.2% for bullion

No dividends nor interest on cash balances are included.

2. In June 1988 the sale was signaled by the FRB Dollar
Index, and the BC read 62 percent and 50 percent for the last
two weeks of May and 67, 61, 58 and 47 percent in June. Selling
into an uptrend required a sale on June 10, 61 percent reading at the first reversal of the most recent positive trend. It's
reflected in the table.

Interestingly, both these two most recent gold transactions
occurred as the Comex price broke through its six-week MA
further confirming the trade.

Figure 8–5 shows the transactions in the bullion market.
The total time invested was 156 months or 60 percent of the
time shown. Nevertheless, the compound gains over the entire
period are 42.4 percent per year for bullion and 49.1 percent for
S&P gold mining stocks.

Perhaps more revealing is the fact that after the gold sale
in March 1980 at $549.12, gold bullion *lost* 25.3 percent of
its price by the end of 1988. But, our back-tested Gold Model produced compound *gains* of 152 percent in bullion and
201.6 percent in gold mining stocks through that same long decline. RMM caught the trading swings dramatically.

LARGEST GAINS

Note the combination of positive LII, CPI, and FRB Dollar Index
signals beginning in November 1975 and extending through
March 1977. This led to the largest gains in both gold itself and
the mining stocks. Another such grouping occurred beginning
in April 1985 and led to the largest gain of the 1980s. Clearly,
when all three signals are on the same side, gold has strong
upside pressure.

It is also important to note that as with stocks and bonds
under the Right Market Method, gold signals require *patience*.
And also the expectation you'll be statisfied not getting market
tops and bottoms. Look at the miss of $250 per ounce off the
peak in 1980, or the approximately 10 percent cuts off the tops
of 1974 and 1987. In trade for this, the Gold Model came very
close to some bottoms: $116 versus $110 in 1976 and $323
versus $300 in 1985 (based on average bullion prices.)

FIGURE 8–5
22 Years of Gold Market Signals vs. Gold Bullion

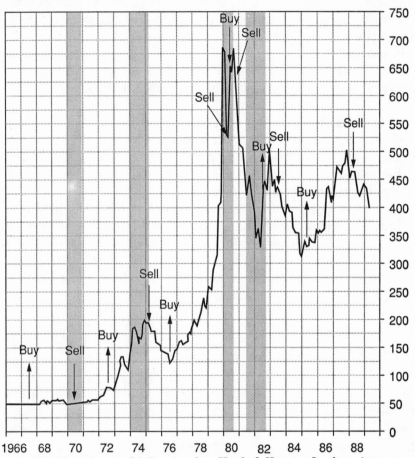

Monthly Averages of daily prices from Handy & Harman. London prices are used prior to 1970. Recession periods are shaded. Graph is based on data through March 1989.

Source: Courtesy of *The Business Picture*, op. cit, Chapter 2.

But the most important investment quality gained is that of not missing any of the largest price moves, the great bull markets. RMM attempts to do exactly this, miss the final peaks and bottoms in order to catch the major moves in between. Believe me, it pays off, even though it causes some frustration as it progresses through trading range markets such as those of

1988 and early 1989. All it's really saying is, "This market may be OK, but it's not the big one you want." If the OK market goes sour, you'll be glad you waited for the rocket.

As to the future, we can be well assured that the Federal Reserve will continue to deal with inflation as a prime enemy, and that this action will be reflected in the markets in the same broad ways as in the past. And we can be very confident that gold will continue to function as a primary inflation hedge as long as the markets for it remain relatively free. Plus, we can be relatively sure that the U.S. dollar will remain the other side of the gold coin. But we can't say that each indicator itself will maintain the same key role in identifying the gold price potential. Indeed, that's why we revised the Gold Model, and why we use multiple indicators, including those that reflect market sentiment and momentum which are not based on economics, but on market participants' real world views. This gives us an economics view and a market outlook combined. To accept less would be ivory tower investing.

THE RULES

We've explained the Gold Model rules generally above, but here they are in detail.

1. When the year-to-year percentage change in both the CPI and LII have a minimum four-month trend that coincides in the same direction, they generate a signal to compare with that of the FRB Dollar Index. Rises in the CPI and LII are positive for gold, while a *decline* in the Dollar Index is also. When all three coincide in direction the strongest gold moves are likely to take place.

2. When the CPI/LII direction is contrary to that signaled by the Dollar Index, the latter overrides and is to be followed. The effect of this in the Model is that the U.S. inflation trend cannot overrule the dollar trend. Instead, it acts as a *buy alert* when both inflation indicators are positive. And it can coincide to prompt the significant gold moves.

3. The Bullish Consensus is used in the same way as for stocks or bonds, to determine market psychology so that sales may be made into bullish sentiment and buys into bearish. The best conditions will be when the BC is hitting new 12-month highs after sell signals and lows after buy signals, but short-term trends in the BC are the conditions most likely to be encountered. Then the same two-week trend signal is used as with stocks and bonds.

4. The moving averages of the gold price are 65 weeks long-term, and 6 weeks for the short-term. The latter is used to confirm transactions in the absence of a clear BC signal. Without either, no buy or sell is made. A breakout through both MAs in a 30-day period overrides all other signals. However, long-term investors may not wish to participate in such volatile and fast action-demanding moves.

5. Since gold mining stocks are about twice as volatile as gold bullion, the best way to control risk in the gold market is to buy bullion or bullion coins *and* gold mining stocks in a 50-50 mixture, (see What To Buy), when the FRB Dollar Index turns *positive*.

On the downside, if the inflation indicators turn negative, we have a sell *alert*. The FRB Dollar Index flashing negative by rising through its nine-month moving average becomes the sell signal, no matter whether the inflation indicators have preceded it or not. This gives the dollar trend a veto over U.S. inflation trends. If our inflation changes are meaningful, they'll show up in dollar movements, anyway.

For those of you who want to develop your own records for these indicators, note that the CPI and LII numbers are reported with at least a month's delay; for example, June numbers are reported in July. Thus, signals from these will actually occur at least five months after a trend begins. Take care in plotting them, especially in conjunction with moving averages. However, the FRB Dollar Index may well cross its nine-month moving average sooner and overcome the inflation indicator wait.

Also, in counting the inflation trend months, they need not be consecutive. Often a reverse trend occurs for a month or two. I skip these reversals and continue the count with the next month *in line* with the original trend. For instance, if February, March, and April are rising months in LII, and May declines, a signal occurs if June's LII number is *above* that for April (the last up month), but not if it's merely above May's level. If the latter happens, wait for the next month to exceed April's level. In fact, it's easiest to chart the monthly changes because the trend is clearer and the count won't be readily mistaken.

WHAT TO BUY

One of the handiest aspects of gold is that there are many ways to buy it for investment. As might be expected, each of the forms in which it is available offers pluses and minuses compared to the others. This does permit investors to choose the form with which they are most comfortable. The rule of thumb is that the closer the gold investment vehicle is to the pure metal, the less volatile is its price. Gold futures and options are then the most volatile and risky paper, and bullion or bullion coins the least so.

Gold bullion is the fundamental form of gold production. It ranges in size from as small as 1/10 ounce up to multi-ounce bars, each graded according to purity in parts of gold per 1,000. 995 is considered the minimum acceptable investment level.

Greatest plus/minus: Bullion's bulk, weight, and need for secure storage usually make this form least practical for investment, although some domestic brokerage firms do provide accumulation programs where the bullion is stored for you. If care is taken in broker selection (some of the greatest scams of the past two decades have been with gold dealers), bullion is a conservative investment form.

Gold bullion coins have become the most popular way to own physical gold over the past dozen years. These are minted for numerous national governments in widely varying weights and denominations of domestic currency. The U.S. one-ounce Eagle and Canadian one-ounce Maple Leaf are the most widely held coin of this type by American investors. Bullion coins usually sell for 3 percent to 5 percent above their pure bullion value, with the exceptions of the South African Krugerrand and Austrian and Hungarian coins.

Greatest plus/minus: Small size and weight make for ease of handling and storage, although security and the cost of it remains a problem for large quantities. Acceptable grading as to wear and marking has been a problem for all gold coins. Again, accumulation programs are available through some brokers.

Numismatic coins are priced on the basis of their age, rarity, and condition, rather than the bullion price. These are collector's items and the subject of a whole investment expertise which makes them especially sensitive to acceptable grading standards, a serious problem in recent years. They are least suitable of the physical gold forms for our purposes due to price movements that tend to be independent of all but extended bull markets in bullion or stocks.

Gold certificates are the evidence an investor receives that a dealer is holding bullion or bullion coins in storage for the owner. With established, reputable dealers/brokers this evidence is satisfactory, but many examples of illegal commingling and outright fraud have developed over these receipts in recent years. Cost of storage and insurance is a factor in holding the gold behind these certificates.

Gold mining stocks are the most easily and widely traded of the gold investment forms. They're available on exchanges and "over the counter" in all countries with such mines. Prices tend to be much more volatile than the bullion price due to operating leverage, and the smaller issues can be highly speculative. Diversification among these stocks is the best way to own them, which is why mutual funds that invest in them make sense.

Gold futures contracts and *gold options* are the most speculative form of gold ownership due to their high leverage and periodic expiration dates. In the contracts leverage stems from low and variable margin requirements set by the exchanges which trade them. In options it arises from the relatively low option price compared to its strike (exercise) price. Only investors who are willing to assume high capital risks should use these forms of gold market participation.

For the purpose of following our gold bull market indicators, most investors will find either the mutual funds listed in Figure 8–6 or the gold bullion or bullion coin purchase programs available through brokers/dealers to be the preferred participation form. Again, exercise particular care to buy bullion/coins from only long-established, highly reputable dealers if you wish them to hold the physical metal/coins for you.

FIGURE 8–6
U.S. Gold Mutual Funds

Fund	Assets 1/31/89 (in millions of dollars)	Sales Charge (%)	Expenses
Benham Gold Equities Index	10.8	none	na
Bull & Bear Gold Investors	40.5	none	high
Fidelity Sel. Prec. Metals	197.0	3(b)	high
Scudder Gold Fund	7.8	none	na
United Services Gold Shares	247.6	none	low
USAA Gold	171.0	none	na
Vanguard Special Gold	128.9	1(b)	low

na = not applicable
b = back-end charge upon redemption of shares

Benham Gold Equities Index Fund is unique among the group in that it is an unmanaged index of 30 North American gold mining stocks. It thus offers the purest play on the mining stock groups and is conceptually ideal for our program. It's operated by the Benham Capital Management Group of Palo Alto, California, which has some $5 billion in other funds under management. The same firm operates Benham Certified Metals, which offers physical gold and bullion coins by accumulation plan or outright purchase.

THE INCOME ISSUE

A final matter, that of income from gold shares, needs to be addressed for those investors who require a regular flow of cash from their investments. Obviously, with gold bullion or futures/options, income is nil unless one uses covered option writing as an income production technique. However, many gold mining issues pay some dividends. Usually they're very modest in yield, as the companies believe they can reinvest their cash flow for a better return in their mining operations than by paying it out to stockholders. Moreover, the mining shares, as we've noted, tend to be quite volatile. Thus, the combination of low dividend payouts and volatility make mining shares generally unsuitable for income investors, and I don't recommend them for that purpose. However, income investors require protection against inflation surges in the economy and worldwide crises as much or more than other investors. For this reason, income investors should purchase *limited amounts* (5 to 10 percent of portfolio) of gold bullion at times of *signaled* gold bull markets, if at all possible.

We've seen how the three sets of key indicators form Models for each of our focus markets, how the sentiment measures can be used to improve (but not guarantee) transaction timing, and how well the Models have functioned over the past two-plus decades. That's almost enough to make us indicator "freaks," as current parlance has it.

However, there is an important distinction between these types of indicators and others that are better called cycles or cyclical tendencies. The two categories are often confused. Next, we'll clear up that difference with a look at some of the more prominent "cycles." Keep in mind how this difference occurs: The indicators we use have a clear relationship between their actions and the conditions that cause the economy or a market to move. As a result they form *irregular* chart patterns, ones that cannot be counted on to show up at a certain future date. Still, their *effect* is reasonably predictable.

Cycles, on the other hand, have a *regular* periodic pattern which is expected to repeat. But it is their effect which is in doubt. Some soothsayers insist the effect is certain. In reality, we'll see just how doubtful that proposition is.

CHAPTER 9

CYCLE CONUNDRUMS

We will not have any more crashes in our time.—*John Maynard Keynes*

I don't know what the famous economist, Mr. Keynes, was using for a crystal ball when he made that comment to Swiss banker Felix Somary two years before the most famous crash in history. Chances are it was some sort of cyclical pattern Keynes thought he'd divined. His statement exudes the sort of certainty that often arises from an apparently everlasting cycle on a chart.

On the other hand, it's unlikely that Keynes was a chartist—the art hadn't been invented in the Twenties—so we'll probably never be certain what prompted his predictive gaffe.

However, it is very rare that mere columns of numbers of such esoteria as employment trends, GNP growth patterns, or consumer debt figures cause fervorous beliefs. But charts and cycles do. They *look* so good they tempt all sorts of otherwise sensible financial thinkers to become sloppy. Therein lies their problem, as we'll see shortly.

So what is the value of looking at cycles? Are there certain cycles that do repeat with such regularity that we can forecast market movements with them?

Many market analysts believe the answer to be yes, including a number of friends who have gained some prominence in following them. However, I submit that the evidence, when carefully analyzed, says that none now known can truly forecast market trends. But this does not make the cycles useless when their limitations are understood. There are certain cyclical patterns that operate periodically in a given market, and we can develop very important information from them.

The history of market cycle use is littered with failed predictions. Most of those apparent cycles certainly don't meet Webster's definition: "regularly recurring successions of events or phenomena." In my reading of that standard, if there are exceptions to the cycle, there is no regularly recurring succession.

So how can cycles be useful? There are several ways in which those that I call "cyclical tendencies" provide market insight:

1. They may overlap with other "tendencies" to be convertible into useful probabilities. For example, the tendency of the business cycle, which is clearly an irregular tendency, becomes interesting when combined with the predictable national election cycle. To be sure, they don't create predictable business turning points, but they do combine to generate a probability range for when recessions are highly unlikely to occur and when they're most likely to happen. If you don't bet the store on them, this can provide a useful insight.

2. Historical relationships, the kind we've defined as market indicators, including the trend in short-term interest rates, periodically interact with cyclical tendencies to yield interesting ideas. For example, we've seen that the degree of FRB monetary tightening has a direct bearing on the probability for a business recession. If we then combine this factor with the election cycle, we find that *if* such monetary tightening occurs within 12 months surrounding an off-year presidential election, the historical probability of recession reaches a very high level. This is not a true cycle, to be sure. Only the election part is cyclical. But the combination is a very valuable tendency to be aware of.

3. Cyclical trends may generate observable patterns that, if a sufficient number of them occur in succession and fit a given theory of why they should occur, can provide excellent market insights. This is the basis of so-called technical analysis using market charts or statistics. One example among many: When a front-weighted average of NYSE advances and declines develops a series of succeedingly *lower* highs, while a market index like the S&P 500 simultaneously develops a series of *higher* highs, an important divergence occurs that is almost invariably resolved by a correction in the *index*, not the advance/decline balance. The theory is that the broad market is likely to sway the narrower index at important turns, rather than the other way around.

There's a negative aspect to apparent cycles that we should be alert to. Very often the best-sounding and widely touted cycles are simply statistically meaningless. We can avoid being caught in their traps by knowing how to check their validity. The best known examples are the infamous Kondratieff Wave and, more recently, the Batra Depression Cycle.

The bottom line on cycles is that since it is virtually certain that no cycle operates with true long-term predictability in the financial markets, or we'd all be rich from using it, we should be wary of claims to the contrary. But, this does not prevent the good use of certain cyclical tendencies to aid in market analysis. Let's consider a few of the better and the worst, some of which I first analyzed in my book, *Low Risk Profits in High Risk Times*.

Investment practitioners appear to be constantly looking for provable cyclical trends. Occasionally they think they've found them.

A catalogue published in the mid-60s listed more than 200 "apparent" stock market cycles, ranging from 20 hours in length to 88 ½ years. Stock market author Burton Crane recalled in his book, *The Sophisticated Investor*, a man who years earlier had operated an advisory service based on events in the comic strips on the *Chicago Sun*.

A few present-day advisors base predictions on astrology or astronomy, including advisory letter editor, Arch Crawford, who did manage to call the stock market top in 1987. Unfortunately, that seems to have been a rather rare hit. No matter. Sunspots, phases of the moon and the planets, and the "Jupiter Effect" have been cited by other market gurus as reasons for expecting a given market event. These sorts of financial predictions have often had the regretable effect of making astrology look good.

These advisors know (at least I think they do) that if someone could locate a prefectly repeating cycle, the probability would be that the next cycle turn would invalidate it. Advisors all hedge their bets on their "cycles" history.

There are a handful of investment cyclical tendencies that have appeared to have something more going for them. One is a monthly stock market cycle that from the mid-60s through 1980 showed a tendency for the S&P 500 to rise from the last day of a month through the fourth day of the next. But, taking a recent example, in calendar 1988, it batted 75 percent *in error.*

Far better is the pre-holiday seasonality in stocks. The two trading days prior to each of the nine annual public holidays has a bullish success approaching 80 percent, according to author/advisor Norman Fosback in *Stock Market Logic.*

Advisor Yale Hirsch insists in Stock Traders Almanac that Mondays at any time of the year have such a tendency to decline that investors should never plan to sell stocks that day.

On the other side of the coin is the apparent cycle that has no conceivable basis for existing but works anyway. The Super Bowl Predictor is probably the best example. It claims that the annual Super Bowl winner, based solely on the original football conference of the winning team, can predict the stock market trend for the year. Winners from the old NFC are bullish.

Through 1988 this cycle had predicted 20 out of 22 years correctly using either the NYSE Index or the S&P 500 as the market measure.

This is pure post hoc reasoning. Clearly the Super Bowl and the NFL can have no operative connection to the stock market. So the predictor should be no better than a coin toss. But there are a couple of facts that give it an historical predictive edge. First, there are more NFL franchises that come from the old NFC than from the AFC, and more NFC teams have won the Super Bowl than AFC teams. Second, the stock market has been up 16 of the last 22 years anyway. The rest of the predictor's apparent success can be explained by a "run," that is, the number of times a coin toss comes up heads or tails in a row before the true probability of 50-50 takes hold. Scratch one predictor.

The so-called January barometer for stocks reveals other problems to be aware of in discovering apparent cycles. This supposed cycle says the stock market trend in January will be matched by the rest of the year. As sinple as that appears, consider the difficulties this statement creates.

First, the barometer is usually used by taking the January trend, up or down in the averages, and forecasting the whole year, January through December from it. But, what if January was up ten percent and the whole year showed a gain of five percent, for example? January did correctly call the year's trend, up. But, of what use was it? February through December had to *decline* five percent to achieve a net five percent rise for the year. Besides, there's nothing like getting a running start on your year's call with 1/12 of your measurement already in the book.

A second problem with this same indicator occurs if we use the indicator fairly, that is, to call the February through December trend once January's is known. As it turns out, this has been a splendid indicator since shortly after World War II. Of the 40 years through 1988, January's trend correctly called 32 of the February through December periods. That's 80 percent correct.

Astutely, however, you might notice that this was an era covering some of the great bull markets in history. That would lead to a logical question: What would the record be if one simply forecast *every year* to be an up year? Oops. That would have gotten 30 of the 40 right. The January barometer was worth exactly five percentage points more than a bullish stopped clock.

What's worse, going back to 1925, January forecast the balance of the year correctly less than *one-half* the time through 1947. So much for the January barometer.

The lesson from analyzing just a few apparent cycles is that very few stand up to sound tests. One of the most famous falls under its own weight.

THE KONDRATIEFF WAVE

A Russian name has become prominently associated with cycles, especially in the doom-and-gloom crowd where fatalism seems to prevail. Nikolai Kondratieff was an economist who attempted to prove, through papers published in 1922 and 1926 in the Soviet Union, that capitalist economies behave cyclically in conjunction with a so-called long wave of 45 to 60 years duration, centering on 54 years. Specifically, he said that this wave applies to prices, interest rates, and economic production in major industrial nations.

Many economists and economic soothsayers have taken up his cudgel since his late 1920s banishment to Siberia. Whenever a serious recession strikes the western industrialized world, they trot out his theory in an attempt to pinpoint that slump's location on the long wave. It seems that the worse the economic slump, the closer these folks believe the world is to the major downleg in Kondratieff's wave.

Because of the world-wide attention given to it, the Kondratieff Wave is an intriguing cycle to examine. Extensive attempts have been made to prove or disprove the theory, notably in the negative by economists C. Van Ewujk in the Netherlands and John A. Pugsley in the United States. Notable proponents are investment advisor Julian Snyder and MIT Professor Jay W. Forrester.

I find three significant fallacies with this wave.

Inaccurate Prices

The first problem with the Kondratieff Wave, commonly seen in an idealized form compared with a chart of U.S. wholesale prices, is that the prices that made up a key element in the wave theory show great variability.

To see this problem, compare the wave with the price chart used by Kondratieff himself in 1935, which is shown in Fig. 9–1.

FIGURE 9–1
The Kondratieff Wave vs. U.S. Wholesale Prices

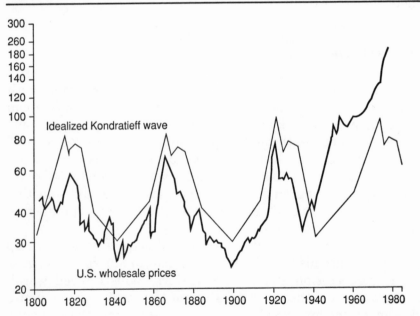

Notice first the magnitude of the change on the "idealized" wave graph from about 1870 to just before 1900: It falls from approximately 83 to 30 on the scale, about 64 percent. On Kondratieff's 1935 chart, the U.S. wholesale price figure drops from about 70 to under 25. That's a greater percentage decline–over 78 percent. Perhaps one of the charts just got the numbers wrong or the magnitude of change doesn't count, only the direction does.

Then note that the idealized wave itself completely lacks a secondary and flatter downleg around 1940 similar to the ones from about 1825 to 1840 and from 1880 to 1900. If it had such a leg, the low would be out near 1955, quite a distance from the low in wholesale prices that the chart and real-world facts show to be in 1933.

Both the actual and idealized graph lines agree that a peak in U.S. prices occurred about 1920, so how could the real low in 1933 have happened? That would make the previous cycle stretch only from the 1896 low (where Kondratieff stated it occurred) to 1933. A period of only 37 years, not the 45 to 60 years that Kondratieff expected. Was it sort of a "short" long wave?

Another problem with the chart is that only *two* trough-to-trough wholesale price cycles exist, and one of them (as just noted) is suspect. Is the wave to be a "long" wave of about 50 years followed by a "short, long" wave of under 40 years? Possible of course, but that fact cannot be determined by a chart of so few cycles.

Period Studied

The matter of cycle duration causes another problem. Drawing sound conclusions about the validity of a cycle based on finding physical evidence requires a significant number of cycles. The appropriate number is arguable. Economist Pugsley notes that one expert requires the period studied to be 10 times the length of one apparent cycle. There is general agreement that a minimum of a half dozen apparent cycles need to be compared. Yet, in Kondratieff's case the *maximum* number of cycles observed in the 36 statistical series he measured was 2½. Moreover, that many cycles were found in only four series of data he used. The rest had fewer cycles, and 11 sets covered only *one* cycle.

If all this weren't enough, the individual contributions of each of those 36 series are a bit unusual. They cover a wide range of variables, from prices to interest rates and production levels to consumption rates, but the eight that were of the maximum 2 or 2½ cycles in length were all *monetary* series (i.e., related to prices and interest rates). Of the remaining 28, seven of which were also monetary, fully 10 *showed no cyclical action at all*, and 18 revealed no more than 1½ cycles.

In sum, the Kondratieff wave theory is based on drawing correlations (and not statistical ones at that) where less than *one-fourth* of the data series studies covered even two full cycles, which is about one-third that widely accepted minimum for valid comparisons, and all of these were monetary indicators, not production or consumption series.

One could argue that some sort of long-wave cycle might exist in monetary measures, but Kondratieff's evidence didn't prove it, let alone extend it to whole economies, as his proponents claim. Kondratieff himself stated in his paper *Long Cycles in Economic Conditions*, delivered in 1926, "Although the period that was studied, covering a maximum of 140 years, *is too short to permit definitive conclusions*, the existence of long cycles would appear to be, at the very least, extremely likely" (italics mine).

I believe a more accurate statement would be that over the period studied, some data suggest the existence of a "long cycle" in financial matters of a few capitalist countries (England, Germany, France and the United States). Such a cycle can be neither proved nor disproved from the data. Its demonstrated variability in length and form, plus the changes in the world economy since the 1930s, make forecasting any future reoccurrence absolutely unreliable. But, it's an interesting idea.

By the way, finding cycles that "work" doesn't mean you can make money from them. Cycle researchers Norman Fosback and Ian McAvity have each stressed that despite the apparent strong degree of predictability of some cycles, basing actual transactions in the marketplace on them are too often not profitable. The real world raises such defeating problems as finding the right vehicle, the cost of broker commissions, effective market executions, and exact timing of the trades.

THE GREAT DEPRESSION OF 19??

The most recent popular book that deals with cycles is the 1987 best-seller, *The Great Depression of 1990*. It was written by Dr. Ravi Batra, Professor of Economics at Southern Methodist University.

I find faults similar to those of the Kondratieff Wave in Batra's thesis. Among the most important are exceptions in the cycle and too few series used to be meaningful. But when I asked Professor Batra on my syndicated radio program if his cycles were statistically significant, he replied, "They're the best evidence we have." Well, if the best is insufficient, should we use it?

The basis of Batra's theory is that two sets of data, one financial and the other governmental, have a similar, but not identical pattern since the 1770s. Each allegedly identifies a 30-year cycle through the 1970s, in which the lows resulted in depressions. Indeed, the charts accompanying his discussion look remarkably alike. But closer analysis reveals problems. See Figures 9–2 and 9–3.

The first data pair is that of money growth and the inflation rate. This connection between the two is vintage Milton Friedman and his *Monetary History of the United States*: Growth and contraction of the money supply prompts surges and declines in the rate of inflation. While the timing connection between the action and reaction may be somewhat loose, many economists believe the theory to be very solid.

Batra's charts of this connection do have cyclical peaks every 30 years or so, but with one notable exception, 1890. This is followed by a new 30-year pattern starting in 1910, with cyclical lows in the 1930s and 1960s, and presumably in the 1990s. Thus, one argument for the "Depression of 1990."

Quibbles begin with the fact that the deflation of the 1930s persisted until World War II and that the next actual deflation occurred 13 years later, in 1954, not the 1960s, which is better known for its inflation than deflation. Still, Batra projects the next deflation low in the 1990s.

Those problems aside, we have in this pair of data series four peaks and three troughs from 1770 to 1860, an interrup-

FIGURE 9–2
Long-Run Cycles of Inflation and Money Growth per Decade (1750s–1970s)

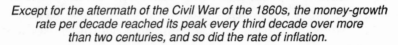

*Except for the aftermath of the Civil War of the 1860s, the money-growth
rate per decade reached its peak every third decade over more
than two centuries, and so did the rate of inflation.*

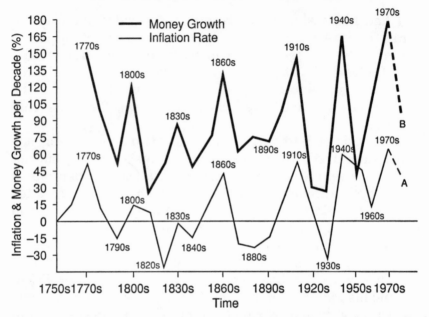

Source: *The Great Depression of 1990* by Dr. Ravi Batra; Simon & Schuster. Used
with permission.

tion or extended bottom in the 1880s through the 1890s, and a
new pair of three peaks and two troughs from 1910 through the
1970s.

Batra explains the 1880s–90s interruption as the "aftermath of the Civil War" and says it's a phenomenon that forced
the next cyclical low to become exaggerated—the lowest low of
the cycles.

To list just a few of the statistical and logic problems with
this claim:

1. Why was the Civil War the cause of the 1880s–90s
superlow in inflation? Why not the great gold discoveries that
began in 1849 and ran through the 1860s, and resurged in the

FIGURE 9-3
The Long Run Cycles of Regulatory Growth in the United States (1760–1980)

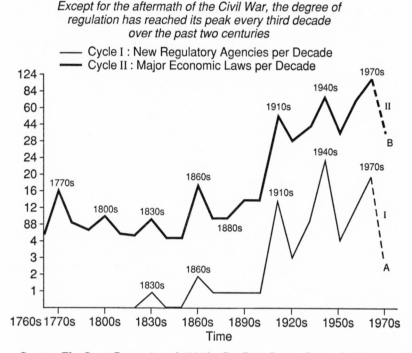

*Except for the aftermath of the Civil War, the degree of
regulation has reached its peak every third decade
over the past two centuries*

—— Cycle I : New Regulatory Agencies per Decade
—— Cycle II : Major Economic Laws per Decade

Source: *The Great Depression of 1990* by Dr. Ravi Batra; Simon & Schuster. Used with permission.

1890s? As they tended to be inflationary periods, a deflationary low between them would have better theoretical connection to his data on monetary growth and inflation.

2. If we accept the Civil War cause, is another such war then necessary to create Batra's forecast of a superlow in the 1990s? If not, why not?

3. What basis is there for saying that four peaks and three troughs, followed after an aberration by three peaks and two troughs resembles a cyclical pattern? There clearly is not a reasonable uninterrupted minimum of a half dozen or more cycles. There's no uninterrupted pattern at all. The inadequacy in number of cycles isn't as bad as Kondratieff's, but it's still insufficient.

4. The thesis for this alleged cycle can only be acceptable on the evidence if the 1880s–90s break is considered part of the pattern. But if that is to be so, the pattern before the break must equal that after it. If it did we are due another *moderate* trough in the 1990s to match that of the 1860s, plus a new peak, BEFORE the next superlow. This pattern would then match the four peak–three trough pattern prior to the 1880s.

The second set of data series has, to be sure, a very similar pattern to the first set, except it is made up of totally different bases: the number of new regulatory agencies and the number of new economic laws. It certainly is interesting that these appear to peak and bottom every 30 years or so and exhibit the same extended low in the 1880s and 1890s as the monetary data. But what is the connection between the two pairs of data? Batra bases it on an old social theory from India. I believe most logic experts would agree that two unrelated sets of data that appear to coincide in chart pattern is better explained by coincidence than a mysterious eastern social relationship. In any case, the regulatory series' have the same faults as the monetary pair noted above. Plus the chart shows regulatory agencies weren't even countable until just before the 1820s, which gives its chart only two peaks and one trough before an 1870s–90s lower plateau.

But, there's more—as though more were needed. A connection is needed to economic depressions in Batra's reasoning. It's the end-point of the Batra exercise; 1990 is to be a depression year, not just a deflationary one.

Batra says that depressions also show a 30-year cycle, a skipped low and another 30-year depression low. Let's accept his statement that one occurred in the 1780s, missed the 1810s, hit the 1840s *and* the 1870s, missed the 1900s and flattened the 1930s. That pattern is hit, miss, hit, hit, miss, hit, X? From what we are shown to this point the X should have occurred in the 1960s and should have been a depression hit, matching the double hit in the 1840s and 1870s. But, the 1960s clearly missed a depression. Batra says this is part of the pattern. Each skipped 30-year low calls for a stronger hit 30 years after the miss, for example, in the 1990s.

I submit that this breaks the pattern shown, and if it were to be true, there simply aren't enough data points to prove it.

Finally, we need only compare the actual economic depression lows of the 1780s, 1840s, 1870s, and 1930s to see that they do not coincide with the lowest lows in the four data series on the charts shown. Two of the depressions, the 1840s and 1870s, were at *interim* lows in all four data charts.

The trouble with all of this, then, is that while there *appears* to be some sort of 30-year cycle operating in the four data series, it is not regular, it coincides with severe economic dislocations only half the time, and the pattern the whole melange develops is far better explained by coincidence than a cycle in operation.

A depression may indeed develop in 1990. But this thesis has not met any sound test in predicting it.

THE POLITICAL CYCLE

Figure 9–4 combines short-term interest rates, stock prices, and inflation with elections and recessions for the inflation-deflation era 1966–88. This chart gives the strongest graphic evidence behind the claim that Washington is the principal creator of our economic roller coaster. Let's see how good its support is.

The evidence suggests a distinct four-year influence is at work on both stock prices and interest rates. Studies of the stock market averages going back to 1917 have found a pronounced tendency toward a four-year cycle. Of 16 full cycles since then, 10 have been four years, only 2 were three years, and 4 were five years long.

During the most recent inflation era shown in the chart, the stock market cycle clearly tended to peak in presidential election years and to bottom in congressional election years. Since 1968, four stock market tops have occurred at or within a few months following the four presidential elections. The four succeeding congressional election years saw bottoms or interim lows in the stock averages within three months of the election–except when the low preceded ballot day by just over four months in 1970. In fact, since 1947 there has been a significant series of ten *consecutive* bear market lows in stocks reached within 12 months of midterm congressional elections. That's one of the better cyclical records around.

FIGURE 9–4
Stocks, T-bills and Inflation, 1966–89

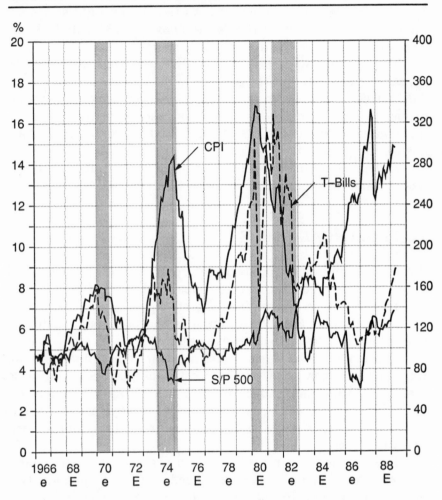

Monthly averages of daily closing yields. Recession periods are shaded. Graph is based on data through March 1989. Three-Month Treasury Bill Rate yields are quoted on a bank-discount basis.

CPI, year to year % charges are based on current month over year earlier month.

e = Congressional election year

E = Presidential election year.

Source: Courtesy of *The Business Picture.*

Also interesting during this era was the tendency for price inflation, as shown by the CPI, to be at or approaching its lows in presidential election years (1968, 1972, and 1976), while highs or proximities to them were seen in midterm years of 1970, 1974, 1978, and 1986. Short-term interest rates tracked the inflation pattern closely, except for an added cyclical low in 1980.

Finally, as might be expected from the foregoing, three of the four recessions of the past dozen years began *after* presidential elections and were over before the next; but they were in full swing or ending as Congress went before the voters in 1970, 1974, and 1982. The exception was the Carter blunder of 1980.

Thus, empirical evidence suggests that an election cycle is working within our economic framework, and it is certainly based on a compelling theory: the need for politicians to put a best financial face forward when appealing to voters. It is not surprising that each presidential administration swings the greatest weight in this historical cycle, not Congress. These facts make the political cycle useful in dealing with markets, but it must be used with care. Remember 1980.

As a weather vane, such a broad pattern as the political cycle should tell us in which direction to look, but *not what to do*. This is especially so because the cycle has a high potential for being disrupted if the economy doesn't respond properly or on time to the politician's exhortations. The "what to do and when" part is properly identified through other, more sensitive market-oriented indicators. One, as noted earlier, is short-term interest rate trends.

As Figure 9–5 shows, short-term interest rates peaked between 3 and 14 months *before* each midterm election since 1966, while the stock market bottomed within 9–14 months either side of the same election. In fact, a major stock market low occurred in *every* midterm election year, or within two months of it, since 1952, except for 1986. Thus, looking for an interest rate decline and stock market upturn would have been wise in almost all those seven midterm election years.

Another element of testing for any indicator must be its profitability. Here the stock market reaction to politicians is very instructive. If investors could have bought the S&P 500 Index, or stocks that performed equally to it, and done so just

FIGURE 9–5
Short-Term Interest Rate Peaks versus Midterm Elections

Mid-Term Election Year	Interest Rate Peak	Major Stock Market Low
1966	Within 3 months	October 1966
1970	Within 11 months	May 1970
1974	Within 3 months	October 1974
1978	None	March 1978
1982	Within 14 months; a secondary peak within 9 months	August 1982
1986	An interim peak within 9 months	Interim Sept. 1985 Low Oct. 1987

at the average level of the index in congressional election years and sold at the index average of presidential years, some very nice gains would have resulted. There would have been not one losing sequence since 1946–48. The average two-year gain would have been 28 percent. Not bad.

It was not easy to buy the S&P 500 itself prior to 1975, but it can now be done with an index fund or an index futures contract. Picking the average level for the year is more difficult, but selecting an arbitrary buy point that's equal to one-half the average percentage range of these prior congressional and presidential election years (1950–1988) ought to get you in the ball park.

Of course, this is a cyclical tendency, not a true cycle, but it has good logic and a moderate history going for it. Plus, almost brainless effort.

There's a corollary to this tendency that's even more interesting. It's the downside of the same political pattern: the irregular business cycle in relation to the regular election cycle.

Figure 9–6 shows the presidential election years since World War II and the subsequent peak of economic activity. Only three elections were not followed by recessions starting or continuing within a year: 1964, 1976, and 1984. (The 1988 cycle is incomplete at this writing.) Predicting downward pressure on the economy to occur just before or after each presidential election would have been correct seven of ten times, a reasonable batting average.

Profiting from this knowledge is more problematic. The stock market, having a tendency toward peaks in presidential

FIGURE 9–6
Election Cycle Stock Market Gains Using S&P 500 Index
Average Levels

Year	S&P 500 Average Level	Percentage Gain
1950	18.40	
1952	24.50	33.1
1954	29.69	
1956	46.62	57.0
1958	46.24	
1960	55.85	20.8
1962	62.38	
1964	81.37	30.4
1966	85.26	
1968	98.70	15.8
1970	83.22	
1972	109.20	31.2
1974	82.55	
1976	102.01	23.6
1978	96.02	
1980	118.59	23.5
1982	119.7	
1984	160.5	34.1
1986	238.9	
1988	267.0	10.5
	Average	28.0%

years and lows in congressional election years, is bound to be far less cooperative in postpresidential election years. It rose in only three of ten postwar, postpresidential election years before 1989.

Gold stocks did somewhat better, having had bull markets in the 1961, 1965, 1973, 1977 and 1985 postpresidential election years, but trouble abounded in the 1969 and 1981 editions of that cycle.

Thus, we have in the election and business cycles a series of useful probabilities arising from sound theory. But they vary considerably in observed results. Accordingly, these "cycles" are fine for orientation, but poor outright forecasters or directors of actions.

We've now analyzed a few of the flaws in how cycles and waves are believed to work. From this, we can say that at a minimum, any apparent cyclical trend should meet at least four criteria to be considered useful:

1. It is supported by a sound economic or investment theory that says it should exist.
2. It is verifiable over a sufficient number of apparent cycles to establish good probability for repetition, preferably a minimum of six. Each must contain the same pattern.
3. Its principal strength does not arise because it is one of multiple cycles with varying lengths arising from the same data.
4. It produces forecastable results that are significantly better than a "stopped clock" prediction.

In accepting these criteria, we must remember that useful information can be garnered from cyclical tendencies, even if they are not perfect cycles.

The key point in this chapter's discussion is the difference between "indicators," as we've used them, and "cycles" as shown. No matter the apparent relevance of a cycle to a series of events, I've never found one that has both a theoretical connection between them and a sound number of historical repetitions. Good indicators have both. Again, this does not mean that apparent cycles cannot provide useful information, as long as it does not prompt firm predictions and action based on them.

In fact, the easiest way to spot the caution point with a cycle compared to an indicator is to look at the chart pattern. If it is a regular cycle repeating a pattern, be wary. Chances are its connection to real-world events is tenuous at best. But, if the pattern is irregular in itself, and sound evidence exists of a cause/effect relationship to the economy or a market, it should warrant further investigation. I believe our indicators fit the latter pattern and their back-testing and real-time use proves they have a great deal going for them.

Finally, it must be stressed that no matter the statistical or real-time evidence of indicator success, there is simply no way they can be guaranteed for the future. Remember the gold market's changes of indicators in the past 25 years. Whistling lemons insist that truth now could be untruth in the future.

CHAPTER 10

ASSET ALLOCATION
AND INVESTOR TIPS

Propagandists, from Shakespeare to Jacqueline Susann, have been telling the unrich that money doesn't buy happiness. The unrich, not being immune to spasms of common sense, sometimes wonder about this.–*Anthony Haden-Guest*

It was about six months after the 1978 publication of my book on foreign tax havens that an intriguing letter arrived. It was from a man we'll call Mr. Black telling me that he'd read the book with much interest and complimenting me on certain details I'd written about the Channel Island of Sark.

The section he liked observed that Sark was the site of the United States' greatest insurance scam, about which I'd said, "The wholly notional Bank of Sark, with an 'audited' balance sheet of $72 million, was identified as administrator and guarantor of multimillions of equally fictional insurance company assets." It seems the fake bank had been used to float a batch of paper which had subsequently been cashed in, creating huge losses for the U.S. insurance companies it was sold to.

Mr. Black's letter concluded with two comments: He was enjoying the wrap-up of his present stay at a place called "La Tuna" (better known as the Federal Correctional Facility in Texas) and second, he'd like to discuss joining *my* organization when he was paroled in a few months. I guess he thought my tax haven knowledge would be useful in his next "project." I've got to hand it to Mr. Black, the man who had perpetrated the Bank of Sark job, for *chutzpah*. And no, we didn't even discuss his joining my firm.

I trust the revelations in this book won't prompt any folks of less than forthright objectives to ask to "assist" in developing a Right Market Method investment vehicle. RMM is legit, and we're full up.

But I do hope that the facts presented here for the first time are sufficiently strong to prompt you to use them in your own investment management. Their potential is certainly significant.

To do this properly, we now must address the linchpin of our approach, which is the specific Asset Allocation Plan. Let's look for a moment at Figure 10–1, the Stock, Bond & Gold Models' Composite Signals, 1967–1989.

Note first that with the exception of 1985 through early 1987 there was no period where all three markets were in bull phases for as long as two years. In fact, there were only two periods where *two* markets were jointly in bull phases for longer than *one* year: 1975–76 and 1982–83. The tendency of this method is alternation among the bull markets, although not frequently. RMM only signaled 38 times in just over 22 years, or well less than twice per year.

While this pattern could change any time, it suggests that asset allocation among the markets need not include holding extensive cash reserves at the first bull market signal, awaiting the next. Wanting to get the most from our money suggests the same idea. Investing maximum cash in the first bull market signaled thus makes best sense. We can then reduce that market position when and if a second or third bull is signaled while the first rolls on.

Secondly, we must follow the rules already given for each bull market signal in allocating funds between bull markets. That is, with stocks we invest in lower-risk vehicles at the initial bull signal. That means stocks or stock funds with risk factors of 70 percent to 90 percent of the overall market. Higher-risk investments are made at the confirmed bull market signal in stocks, (a +3 reading in the Model) to take advantage of the strong gain potential that occurs thereafter.

In gold, we place half the gold segment in bullion/bullion coins and half in the gold mining stocks at the bull market signal. We then retain the 50–50 mixture throughout. With bonds there is no such risk balance at either its first or second

FIGURE 10–1
Composite Bull/Bear Market Signals in Stocks, Bonds, and Gold, 1967–89

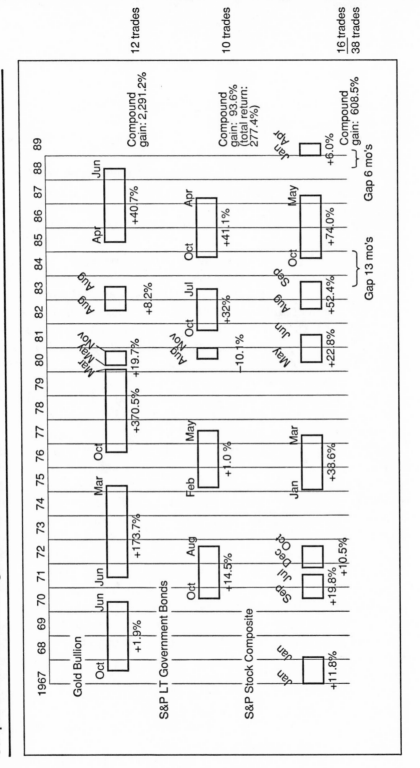

buy signals, but there is a 50 percent bond position reduction upon the first negative signal.

Combining these thoughts, our Asset Allocation Plan is as follows:

1. Upon the first bull market signal from an all-cash position, invest 100 percent of cash in the appropriate bull market vehicles. (See respective chapters for vehicles.) Only if you aren't sure of the signal or have other doubts should this percentage be reduced.

2. The second, confirming bull market signal in *stocks* tells you to increase your risk exposure for maximum gain potential by acquiring higher volatility stocks and stock funds. This should not involve a change in percentage of assets invested, but rather a switch from lower-risk to higher-risk vehicles. Only if you're underinvested should the asset percentage increase. Note that in gold and bonds, no change is made in *risk exposure* at this signal.

3. If a second bull market is signaled while the first is underway, split total invested assets 50-50 between the two by selling one-half your first bull market position. Use lower-risk vehicles in the stock market if it's the first signal of a second bull market, no matter what the stage of the first market is.

4. If a third bull market then arrives while the other two are progressing, take funds *equally from each* of the first two to split capital ⅓ in each of the three bull markets. Again, use lower-risk vehicles in the third bull market if it's stocks, irrespective of the stage of the first two bulls. This balance achieves good diversification while participating in all bull markets.

5. Taking profits will be done in the same way. Do note that the first negative signal (Model readings moving from +3 to +2), are *not* outright sell signals in stocks or in gold unless it's the FRB Dollar indicator for gold. In stocks the first negative is a risk reduction signal, requiring a switch back to lower volatility holdings. In gold, no action is required unless its an FRB Dollar Index negative, which *is* a SELL. In *bonds*, the Model rules say that a reversion from a +3 to +2 reading requires sale of *one-half* your long-term bond position. The proceeds go to cash equivalents.

The first active *sell* signal in stocks is when the Model reaches a reading of +1. This means, you'll recall, that you begin selling all your holdings into market strength. In gold, a second negative signal will again depend on which indicator is doing the signaling. If it's the FRB Dollar Index, it's an "all out" signal. If it's an inflation indicator, you'll treat it as an alert until the final FRB Index signal.

A reduction to a +1 Model reading in bonds is the all out signal, when the remaining one-half of the long-term bond position is sold, with proceeds going to cash.

6. The final position in each market is when the Model reading drops to zero, when *all* long positions are liquidated to ride in a money market fund until the first positive signals again arise.

Keep the above rules handy for your investments decisions, and refer to them regularly until they're fully comfortable. As indicated, limited personal judgment can be exercised with asset allocation percentages because you'll only be reducing or increasing your exposure to a given market, not deciding to stay out or get in. The individual market rules determine that. But these allocation steps were arrived at after considerable thought as to risk control and capital growth potential, so they should not be modified lightly.

A sample of the 1984–1988 market transactions from Figure 10–1 and respective chapters shows the allocation process is clear-cut.

October 1984 Stock Model +2: BUY stocks/funds with relatively lower risk and 50 percent of assets, due to Bond Model also signalling +2: BUY long-term bonds/funds with 50 percent of assets.

December 1984 Stock Model +3: (Not shown.) Switch to aggressive stocks/funds.

April 1985 Gold Model positive (FRB Signal): BUY gold bullion and gold mining stocks (50-50 mix) with 50 percent of money already invested in the stock and bond markets. Asset balance is now ⅓ each market.

October 1986 Stock Model down to +2: (Not shown.) Switch to lower-risk issues from aggressive.

February 1987 Bond Model +2, down from +3: (Not shown.) SELL ½ position in long bonds, proceeds to money market fund.

April 1987 Bond Model +1: SELL other ½ of long bonds,
proceeds to money fund.
May 1987 Stock Model +1, down from +2. Begin to SELL
stock position into strength, proceeds to money fund. Total
position eliminated in three market move steps of 5 percent
each, by August 1987.
June 1988 Gold Model FRB Signal: SELL gold bullion/
stocks, proceeds to money fund.
January 1989 Stock Model up one to +2: BUY lower-risk
stocks/funds with 100 percent of assets.
April 1989 Stock Model down to +1: SELL stocks/funds.

The total gain for the eight basic position changes was 161.8
percent *plus* bond and money fund interest and dividends on
stocks. For ease of illustration, gain also assumes no switch in
stock volatility, no gold mining stocks bought, and no 50 percent
sales in bonds. A buy-hold strategy in the S&P 500 Index gained
87.9 percent plus dividends.

It would certainly appear that the RMM strategy was worth
the switching during this most active period in our entire 22 years
studied. That gain approached *double* that of a buy-hold in the
best single market performing market of the period.

By now it shoud be clear that the Right Market Method is
a strong discipline. It should cover nearly every possible market
contingency and turn because it ignores them until the correct
alignment of indicators signals "go."

As I've also stressed, this investment approach requires waiting out the indicators. The August to December period in 1984
is a good example: Stocks burst on the upside in August, sensing
a decline in interest rates, only to deteriorate through the rest
of the year. Our Stock Model buy signal was acted upon by my
Low-Risk GROWTH Letter in October, and still there was a wait
to year-end before the market soared again. But, the wait paid
off in being positioned for the great bull market of the next 18
months.

Further, asset allocation requires that the investor using it
realize that a switch from one market to another is not always
made because the first market is about to decline. In fact, the
switch usually occurs with some rise left in the initial market
because the indicators aren't trying to pick tops. They're designed
to show where the best opportunity is, not where the last buck is.

You do need the discipline not to fret over a market that's been sold out of but is still rising. Remember, history says the new market should do better, shortly.

A final note for income investors. We've already specified asset allocation rules for income investors in each specific market chapter, and concluded that the bond market is the best one to follow for maximizing income. We've also noted that when the Gold Model turns bullish it would be wise for income investors to shift 5 percent to 10 percent of their portfolio to gold for protection, even though it will mean a cut in income.

For those who wish to use stock income for eventual growth in both capital and income, the asset allocation rule should be to follow the Stock and Bond Models exactly as in the Plan above, shifting concentration as the bull phases change. But be sure to follow the Bond *Income rules* when shifts are made in this market.

What about taxes, you might ask. Even though the switches into the various bull markets aren't frequent, they will require paying tax on any gains. My advice is to pay the tax without major effort to "shelter" it. The returns we've discovered to be possible with RMM are sufficiently above a buy-hold strategy that paying the tax on a current basis should still put you well ahead of leaving gains intact for some future tax collector. Certainly, if you have the option of using RMM in a tax-deferred plan, that will be a plus, although it is no longer possible to assume a lower tax bracket at some future withdrawal date, say retirement, than your current one. The 1989 tax brackets are about as low as we'll ever see, despite the fact that for most investors they can hardly be considered low in absolute terms.

TEN TIPS

Our studies of this investing method have brought out a number of important points that should be followed along with the specific market rules and asset allocation. I consider these to be almost inviolate.

1. Most obvious is to use a set of market indicators for all your securities trades and follow them religiously. Hopefully, they'll be the Right Market rules, but if not, use another set. The value of sticking with a discipline is great in the emotion- and opinion-filled last decades of the 20th century. To do this, assure yourself that the indicators truly work to the point where you have confidence in them. Then, rely on them.

2. Don't attribute more to the indicators than they can deliver. For example, the indicators tell us a lot, but how large the gains will be in following them is not on the list. As do all such signals in RMM, the October 1984 buy signals in stocks and bonds said two things clearly: (1) The downside risk in stocks/bonds is low, not nonexistent, and (2) the upside potential is significant, once the markets get the message. They did not say, "look for the Dow to reach 2500" or any such projection. As much as investors like to put targets on their gains, the savvy ones know that no one, least of all the market, has the foggiest idea of how far prices might go. It's amazing how many investors *know* this and often quote price expectations.

3. Don't become impatient with any set of long-term indicators/rules. Believe me, a long-term approach is the best route to successful investing, but it requires ignoring the markets' periodic enthusiasm and panics in order to catch the major moves where the most money can be made. If you need faster action, find a system that tries to give it. I've dwelled on this point enough, so this is a reminder.

4. No investing method can avoid taking a loss now and then. Even RMM took one out of its 19 buy-sell combinations. But, always keep losses small. Every successful professional I know makes this his/her paramount rule. The way to do this is to use protective mental sell stops and act on them when triggered. This is especially important with individual stock holdings, but can be followed with gold and bonds, too. (Recheck the Chapter 6 description for a refresher.) Don't ever allow your loss to become large. Recovery from that can be the most daunting and painful of investing experiences.

5. The other side of the loss control rule is to establish a performance parameter, one that is realistic and practical for your goals. And don't change your game plan unless you fall short of it over the long term. I've suggested the level of 12–15 percent *compounded* per year as being realistic target figure, but only over more than one year. You can try for more or less, but that's a range that should be achievable over time *without* taking significant risks. Remember, though, you'll probably do worse than that some years, and better in some. So use a review period that allows for this. I like a two-year review. It's short enough to not perpetuate a poor plan, but long enough to give a medium long-term investing approach to work. The following table shows 12 percent compounded annually on $1,000 at the end of each 2 years.

2 years	4 years	6 years	8 years	10 years
$1,254	$1,574	$1,974	$2,476	$3,106

This doubles capital in just over 6 years, and more than triples it in 10 years, an excellent *total return* target, including interest and dividends. Check your progress every two years, and don't be distraught if you have missed by a little, say to a return of 9 or 10 percent compounded per year. Twelve percent a year is not a "slam dunk" goal, but if you're not close, you'd better find another approach.

There's a caveat for income intestors. Clearly, your returns will be more subject to the level of interest rates than will those of the multimarket investor. This may make 12–15 percent an unrealistic target, at least until a good bond bull market provides decent capital gains. This is especially so for those of you earning municipal bond interest. In these cases the rule should be to control your risks to your comfort level, and earn the maximum return possible at those risks. Don't concern yourself about a target return per year.

6. This brings up a related point for growth investors. Don't waste your time trying to "beat the market." Not only is it difficult to do, even for pros, but it will focus your attention on shorter-term results, and that's playing Wall Street's game, not necessarily your own. Remember that performance is personal, not arbitrary. Even the 12 percent target above may not fit your circumstances, especially if you're highly risk averse. Set your own target and ignore the media hype on performance.

7. While we're on the matter of returns, do recognize that unless you're a Rockefeller, what counts is *percentage* return on your money, not points or dollar gains. If you don't start with big bucks, dollar or point gains mean nothing. You don't have enough to make them really pay off. A good example is the point gains (or losses) we hear every day for the Dow Industrials. A 40-point gain is supposed to be a big deal. In 1989 that's not even 2 percent, and 2-percent gains in a day are a dime a dozen in market history. The same is true of individual stocks or bonds. A one-point move on an $8 stock is a nice 12.5 percent; on an $80 stock, it's barely worth noting. Ultimately, this matter will get down to dollars, of course, because that's what's spendable. But, while you're getting there, it's percentages that matter most.

8. Don't pay full service commissions unless you need a lot of help and are paying less than about $1,000 per year in brokerage. This isn't to try to beat your broker out of a living, but simply recognizes the fact that you're using our strategy to call the shots and shouldn't need much assistance from a broker. For that, even full service brokers should give you a break. If they won't don't hesitate to use a discount broker. This is especially true if you're getting specific issue selection and timing from our Low-Risk GROWTH advisory or any other one. You're paying for that information once; don't pay twice. The only exception is if you need help, recognize that fact and don't quibble about paying for it. No free lunch and all that.

9. Don't let taxes get in the way of investment decisions. I said this above in a different context, but here I mean it for all types of securities transactions. I know of more investors who've ridden gains up and down to avoid paying the tax than any other type. Taxes aren't pleasant, in fact they're disgusting. But, post-tax reform, it makes more sense to get the tax hit out of the way than to defer/avoid it. Tax rates aren't going any lower, and I doubt that any sensible American thinks they won't go up. So, delaying is a mug's game. Trying to shelter taxes is even worse. Tax shelters are *deferral* devices, not avoidance vehicles. What's the big advantage in deferring if your bracket will probably rise by the time the tax is due? Sure, there can be specific instances where deferral is OK—compounding a *known* return for several years in a retirement plan, is one—but even then, bracket increases could negate a big chunk of the advantage. Pay the tax.

10. Forget touts, trebles, and tontines. You know what a tout is, but trebles and tontines are something else. You should still forget them all. Touts on stocks or takeovers or other ways your brother-in-law knows to make a million aren't worth the time to hear them. There is always the one, like the glass-enclosed dice in Vegas that rolled 27 straight passes on the crap table, that worked. But the next 9999 won't. Why flaunt the odds? Methodology works. Touts don't.

Trebles are variations on touts. Because nobody wants a stock to double any more, treble is the new buzz word. "I know that when XYZ is bought out, it's going to *treble*." When you hear something like that, or even the mundane *double*, remember the stock doesn't know that, and neither does the stock exchange specialist who handles it nor the OTC marketmaker. If they did, it'd be there by now. Why should you know more?

As to tontines, if you're up on your European insurance law, you'll know they're a form of gambling, too. A group of participants in an insurance plan allow their annuities to build up with the last survivor taking all the marbles. See why I said to forget'em?

A final piece of business. In Chapter 2, I said that we'd compare the "hindsight" bull markets with those our indicators had identified, and that "should be revealing as to how practical the indicators truly are."

The record in Figure 10–2 shows we missed only *one* of the hindsight bull markets in the past 22 years, the four-month gold stock run of 1983–84. But, we also profited from two moves in bonds in the early to mid-70s that didn't make the bull market list. Of course, our gains weren't as large as if we'd caught all the exact tops and bottoms in three markets over two decades, a fact that surprises no one.

But, is our compound gain of 2993.3 percent something to be sneezed at? (Based on the Figure 10–1 trades, without cash interest or dividends.) I think not, when the S&P 500 gained less than 1/10 of that over the same time.

I believe my statements in the Introduction were not inaccurate. There IS a bull market every year. And the Right Market Method reveals them.

On the other hand, I have it on very good authority that pork bellies have bottomed and should triple before this contract's expiration. Any takers?

FIGURE 10–2
Market Results 1966–89

	RMM Calls	
Jan. '67 to Jan. '68:	S&P 500	+11.8%
Oct. '67 to Jun. '70:	Gold	+1.9%
Sep. '70 to Jul. '72:	S&P 500	+19.8%
Oct. '70 to Aug. '72:	Bonds	14.5%
Dec. '71 to Oct. '72:	S&P 500	+10.5%
Jun. '71 to Mar. '75:	Gold	+173.7%
Jan. '75 to Mar. '77:	S&P 500	+38.6%
Feb. '75 to May '77:	Bonds	+1.0%
Oct. '76 to Mar. '80:	Gold	+370.5%
May '80 to Jun. '81:	S&P 500	+22.8%
May '80 to Nov. '80:	Gold	+19.7%
Aug. '80 to Nov. '80:	Bonds	−10.1%
Oct. '81 to Jul. '83:	Bonds	+32.0%
Aug. '82 to Aug. '83:	Gold	+8.2%
Aug. '82 to Sep. '83:	S&P 500	+52.4%
Oct. '84 to May '87:	S&P 500	+74.0%
Oct. '84 to Apr. '87:	Bonds	+41.1%
Apr. '85 to Jun. '88:	Gold	+40.7%
Jan. '89 to Apr. '89:	S&P 500	+6.0%

APPENDIX

STOCK INDICATOR SOURCES AND CALCULATIONS

All: Kinsman & Associates, 255 W. Napa St., #206, Sonoma, CA 95476

STIR Index (Proprietary). An arithmetic combination of the weekly average 90-day T-bill yield and federal funds rate, weighted for the Federal Reserve discount rate. All are available from the Federal Reserve Bank of St. Louis, St. Louis, Missouri. The indicator is used in conjunction with 26-week and 45-week MAs. A move of the Index through its shorter MA is an alert, as it signals Fed intent for changed interest rates. A down move through the longer MA is a positive indicator for stocks and bonds. An up move is negative.

Weighted Consumer Price Index (Proprietary). U.S. Bureau of Labor Statistics, Washington, DC for monthly CPI, or most newspapers.

This indicator is calculated by taking (1) the percent change of the current month's CPI, compared with its previous 12 months' average, (2) calculating a 12-month MA of these percentage changes and multiplying it by 2, (3) weighting the most recent four months of this MA at double the first eight, and (4) calculating a second MA from this data.

Then compare the two MAs. When the difference between the two exceeds 5 percent, a signal is generated. If the weighted MA is in excess of the standard MA, it's a rising *inflation signal,* *which is negative* for stocks and bonds. When the reverse is true, with the weighted MA less than the standard MA by more than the 5 percent, this shows a slowing inflation and is *positive* for the two markets.

200-Day Moving Average of the Market. Available each business day for the Dow Industrials and S&P 500 in *Investors Daily*, on newsstands or office in Los Angeles, California.

BOND MARKET INDICATOR SOURCES

Same as for stocks, except:

Nearby T-bond price and 65-week MA. Prices available daily from the Chicago Board of Trade and numerous newspapers for the nearest month's maturity. Use weekly closing price in calculating the 65-week MA. A bond price move of 3 percent through the MA generates the signal.

GOLD MARKET INDICATORS SOURCES

Consumer Price Index. Bureau of Labor Statistics. (see Stock Indicators above.) Also Barron's, on newsstands each Monday, or subscriptions: 200 Burnett Rd., Chicopee, Maine.

FRB U.S. Dollar Index. Federal Reserve Bank of St. Louis: U.S. Financial Data, weekly. P.O. Box 66593, St. Louis, Missouri, 63166-6593.

Leading Index of Inflation. Center for International Business Cycle Research, Columbia Business School, New York, New York (212) 280-2916.

MORE ABOUT RISK

When analyzing the risk in a stock we define that part of the risk that relates to developments with its company as unsystematic risk. It can be eliminated only by sufficient diversification, such as holding something in excess of 25 stocks, for example. All other risk is known as market risk, or *systematic risk*, and it's the risk investors are paid for taking.

To relate this market risk to expected return from a stock, we determine how much relative systematic risk that stock contains. *Beta* is the name given to this result, and it indicates how much a stock has fluctuated compared to the entire market. The minimum time period that should be covered in this calculation is usually three years, although five is commonly used, too.

So, if a stock (or stock mutual fund) has a *beta* of .7, we mean it has fluctuated about 70 percent as much as the market over a recent time period. Presumably, unless something significant occurs with the company, it will continue to show about this much relative fluctuation in the future. That's its relative systematic risk.

The same risk measure is available for stock mutual funds, and it's more reliable if the fund is widely diversified, due to the inherent reduction in nonsystematic risk in the fund compared to individual stocks.

Betas are available for stocks in both the *Value Line* and *Daily Graphs* services, as noted in Chapter Six.

NO LOAD STOCK FUNDS

The funds in Figure A–1 were on our advisory service's Approved List in mid-1989 and should work well in the RMM Stock Model's Early and Confirmed Bull Market Stages, as noted in list. In order to be selected, a stock fund had to have ranked among the top 20 percent in total return over the three years through 1988, as compiled by *Investor's Daily*. It also had to be a no-load fund, as even low loads of 2 percent (with the exception of Fidelity Magellan, which we're citing for comparison purposes) were excluded from our rankings: If you're paying us for advice you shouldn't have to pay someone else, too.

The fund also had to be part of a family to allow telephone switching, including into a money fund. It also had to be a diversified fund and it had to invest exclusively in the U.S. domestic market.

We next looked at the return the fund generated from 1985 to mid August 1989 compared to the volatility it had over the three calendar years covered. Volatility is simply the degree to

FIGURE A–1
No-Load Stock Funds

Fund	Volatility	Initial Minimum	Size (mils)	Call 800-
Growth (Confirmed Bull [+3] Stage)				
*#Fidelity Magellan	Average	$1,000	$10,757	544-6666
*#Scudder Capital Growth	High	1,000	829	225-2470
Boston Capital Appreciation	Average	1,000	546	225-5267
Price New Era	Average	1,000	765	638-5660
Dreyfus Growth Opportunity	Average	2,500	582	645-6561
Aggressive Growth (Confirmed Bull [+3] Stage)				
*#Janus Venture (small co's)	Below Average	1,000	49	525-3713
*#Columbia Special	Very High	2,000	64	547-1037
Growth & Income (Early Bull [+2] Stage)				
*Price Equity Income	Low	1,000	743	638-5660
Vanguard Windsor	Below Average	10,000	7,884	662-7447
*#Vanguard Windsor II	Below Average	3,000	1,872	662-7447
Dodge & Cox Stock	Average	250	100	434-0311
Babson Value	Average	1,000	11	821-5591
Balanced				
*Mutual Shares**	Low	1,000	3,414	448-3863

*Rated our top buy in category
#Superior 1989 appreciation
**Concentrates in takeover and restructuring companies, both debt and equity.
Only three of the funds rated in the top two categories of *Forbes* magazine's latest performance rankings in *both* up and down markets: Fidelity Magellan, Vanguard Windsor and Doge & Cox Stock.
This list does not contain outright buy recommendations. That advice is only given by our advisory portfolio.

which the fund's price fluctuated in comparison to the S&P 500. It's technically known as the fund's *beta*.

We then ranked the funds on a return-for-volatility basis in order to establish those funds that achieved the best returns in excess of T-bills, with lowest volatility. The best bang for the buck, as it were.

We've also shown the volatility itself for each fund. In our definition, Very Low = below 70 percent of the market's volatility; Low = 70 percent to 79 percent of market volatility; Below Average = 80 percent to 89 percent of market; Average = 10 percent below or above market; Above Average = 111 percent to 119 percent of market; High = 120 percent to 129 percent of market; Very High = 130 percent or more of market.

NO-LOAD BOND FUNDS

The funds in Figure A–2 were on our advisory service's Approved List in mid-1989. The long-term funds below should work well with RMM's Bond model +2 and +3 readings. The medium term funds can be used by income investors.

All approved funds have met the following criteria: Top ranking by category for high yield and/or low expenses, better than average total return for the three years through 1988, and telephone switch capability into other funds in same family.

This list is for reference only. Specific buy/sell recommendations are made only by our advisory portfolios.

FIGURE A–2
No-Load Bond Funds

Name	Volat. (1)	Exp (2)	Curr. Yield (3)	Min. Invest.	Name	Volat. (1)	Exp (2)	Curr. Yield (3)	Min. Invest.
Taxable:					*Tax-Exempt:*				
Long-term					*Long-term*				
Corporates					Benham Cal Tx Fr Tr Long	50%	0.64	6.5	1,000
Dreyfus A Bond Plus	50%	0.84	8.4	2,500	Fidelity Muni Bond	50%	0.51	6.6	2,500
Fidelity Flexible Bond	50%	0.66	8.3	1,000	Stein Roe Mangd Muni	50%	0.62	6.4	1,000
Vanguard Invest Grade	50%	.39	9.1	3,000	Vanguard Insurd Muni	50%	0.26	6.9	3,000
Governments					*Medium-Term*				
Benham Tgt Mat. 2000	60%	0.70	7.8	1,000	Benham Tx Fr. Intermed.	25%	0.50	6.0	1,000
Fidelity Gov't Securities	60%	na	7.8	1,000	Scudder Tx Fr Tgt 1993	25%	0.79	5.7	1,000
Vanguard U.S. Treas.	60%	0.79	8.1	3,000	Vanguard Muni Inermed.	25%	0.26	6.7	3,000
Mortgage Backed					Fidelity Ltd Term Muni	25%	0.74	6.1	2,500
Benham GNMA	55%	0.73	9.4	1,000					
Dreyfus GNMA	55%	1.21	8.5	2,500					
Fidelity GNMA	55%	0.93	8.6	1,000					
Vanguard GNMA	55%	0.38	9.3	3,000					
Medium Term									
Benham Cap. Pres. T-Note	37%	0.93	7.4	1,000					
Benham Tgt Mat. 1995	35%	0.70	7.7	1,000					
Vanguard Sht Trm Corp	40%	0.38	8.6	3,000					

Phone Numbers To Use
All are toll-free, 800:

Benham 4-SAFETY
Dreyfus 645-6561
Fidelity 544-6666
Scudder 225-2470
Stein Roe 338-2550
Vanguard 662-7447

NOTE: (1) Volatility shown is the estimated percentage volatility of fund price compared to S&P 500 over two years through 1988. Don't let the low numbers mislead you. All long-term bonds are risky in sharply rising interest rate markets. (2) The expense percent is the annual amount charged the fund for management and/or promotion. But, all funds listed are "no-load" in terms of front or back sales charges. (3) Yield is the 30-day average as of mid August 1989.

ADDENDUM: THOUGHTS ON THE "FOLLY OF TIMING"

In a 1984 article for the *Harvard Business Review*, titled "The Folly of Stock Market Timing,"* an engineer by the name of Robert H. Jeffrey argued that unless a market timer was able to guarantee to exceed 70–75 percent accuracy in stock market buys/sells (using the S&P 500), there was little reason to follow his or her advice. Jeffrey's statistical backup was substantial.

This argument is germane to our discussion of RMM because, arguably, it is a market timing method, albeit a long-term one. But RMM has important differences from those points raised by Jeffrey, not the least of which is that RMM covers two markets other than stocks, plus stocks. No similar timing research has been done on gold and bonds that I'm aware of.

More pertinent, though, is that any asset allocation method is *ipso facto* designed not to time any one market *most* successfully, but rather to achieve a combined timing that will exceed the results of stocks alone, over time. This RMM has done. And that makes the second key point. Its timing accuracy is 18 profitable trades out of 19 attempts, or 94.4 percent. That's well above the 70–75 percent level noted. The only thing that RMM can't do is guarantee that in the future. Indeed, I'd say it's unlikely RMM results will be consistently over 90 percent. But beating 70 percent? I'll have to give you odds.

---

*See *Classics: An Investor's Anthology*, edited by Charles Ellis, 1989, Dow Jones-Irwin, pp. 689–705.

INDEX